WTF!

Life is not always what it seems

David Clark

Published by New Generation Publishing in 2015

Copyright © David Clark 2015
Copyright on news articles Guardian News & Media Ltd and ABC

First Edition

The author asserts the moral right under the Copyright, Designs and Patents Act 1988 to be identified as the author of this work.

The author and publishers have made all reasonable efforts to contact copyright-holders for permission, and apologise for any omissions or errors in the form of credits given. Corrections may be made in future printings.
British Library Cataloguing Publication Data.
A catalogue record for this book is available from the British Library

ISBN 978-1-78507-324-3

All Rights reserved. No part of this publication may be reproduced, stored in a retrieval system or transmitted, in any form or by any means without the prior consent of the author, nor be otherwise circulated in any form of binding or cover other than that which it is published and without a similar condition being imposed on the subsequent purchaser.

www.newgeneration-publishing.com

An Invite, to Eternity by John Clare

Wilt thou go with me, sweet maid,
Say, maiden, wilt thou go with me
Through the valley-depths of shade,
Of night and dark obscurity;
Where the path has lost its way,
Where the sun forgets the day,
Where there's nor life nor light to see,
Sweet maiden, wilt thou go with me!

Where stones will turn to flooding streams,
Where plains will rise like ocean waves,
Where life will fade like visioned dreams
And mountains darken into caves,
Say, maiden, wilt thou go with me
Through this sad non-identity,
Where parents live and are forgot,
And sisters live and know us not!

Say, maiden wilt thou go with me
In this strange death of life to be,
to live in death and be the same,
Without this life or home or name,
At once to be and not to be -
That was and is not - yet to see
Things pass like shadows, and the sky
Above, below, around us lie?

Table of Contents

Introduction 1

Chapter 1 – The girl and the robot: my psychosis 3

Chapter 2 – So tell me sir, what is it like to be a loony? . 15

Chapter 3 – The warning signs – if only someone had told me 39

Chapter 4 – The system is stuffed – you have to take control even when you are not in control 60

Chapter 5 – We are all bipolar – is that not a good thing? 74

Chapter 6 – What next – even if your world collapses, another door opens... 91

Chapter 7 – Take control – and here's how you can do it 105

Annex A The Lime Green Solutions: My Personal Wellbeing Plan 123

Annex B Meetup e-mails 132

Annex C My bookshelves contain the following gems . 154

Dedication

To my mum
Thank you

Acknowledgements

I wish to acknowledge all those who have played a key part in my journey to this point. Without the following people, I would not be here:

- To Deirdre, thank you for everything you have done for me over the past three years, I am truly grateful
- To Linda, you are amazing. Your smile, your compassion, your understanding - the world is a wonderful place with you in it
- To Sue, my Australian mum. Your smile, your laughter, your presence - always warms my heart and makes me glad to be alive
- To City Library, Stonnington Libraries and Camberwell Library - thank you- you have played a key role in my recovery
- To Jane at the Alfred - everything a wonderful and trustworthy psychiatrist should be - thank you
- To my former neighbours, Janice and Paresh, who tolerated me during my madness - is nice to enjoy your company still, though, now I remember everything
- To Centrelink for presenting me with one of the biggest challenges I have ever faced
- To Laura, for being a game-changer and a superstar
- To George, you saved my life for which I will be forever in your debt
- To Daniel, destined for greatness, believe in yourself and you will fly

Preface

We all know someone or have met someone in our journey who has appeared to us a little eccentric, off-beam, or perhaps a tad eccentric. Well, I know I certainly have. The most extreme experience for me was the man on the bus whilst I was living in London who kept hitting his head whilst talking with no concern or desire to interact with those around him. There was also the work I did at a hospital for the mentally ill in Portsmouth back in the mid-1990s - little did I know: walking around the hospital, passing patients lying on the floor, hearing screams and yelling, feeling slightly outside my comfort zone. Oh me oh my, what a journey it has been.

And so to the book. It is a tale of my journey. It is not just about my recent episode of psychosis but a broader insight into life and how we should live every day. I know this may sound a little cliché but I am being serious here - we cannot ever know enough about what is going on inside our bodies and inside our minds. We have the ability to lead wonderful lives.

All the answers are out there. Some are inside this book. All you have to do is take action.

As I often say, life is like taking a plane journey. You start off in economy, travelling light. Then as you grow up, you - consciously or subconsciously - collect baggage. Without knowing, you are in premium economy and then business and when you get to some point in your forties or fifties you arrive in first class, carrying more baggage than a major airline might allow you to fly with. At some point in your life you realise you have to take control and this is what this book is about - taking control. You will become the pilot of your journey, of your life. The question is - when will you decide? It is, after all, your choice. It is your life! Live it to your best potential and whatever you do in life - smile!

Enjoy, Dave

Madness: a memoir by Kate Richards

Mental illness happens to people who are living ordinary, good lives, just like my family and me when I first became ill. And for the families, friends and carers of people with mental illness it is particularly hard because the illness can take away our ability to know that we are loved and we often find it hard to love back in conventional ways. For some of us, after a while we forget how to love.

For me, staying well is a daily job of monitoring mood and thinking and keeping regular rhythms of waking and sleeping. I take medication every morning and evening, and will do so for all of my life. At thirty-eight, I've been well for around four years but I'm not "cured". Good health doesn't come with a guarantee for anyone, but for those of us managing a long-term illness each day of wellness is, in its own way, remarkable.

I'm grateful to be living in a country where medication and therapy are mostly available and affordable. However, in Australia, we are still not caring for the most vulnerable members of our communities: those who, through no fault of their own, are not as lucky as I have been to respond to medication or to be able to afford to find the right kind of therapy. These people are of all ages and background, and we ignore their suffering because most of us don't understand their ways of seeing the world or we are afraid of their differences or embarrassed by their appearance and because we can't see their injuries.

No-one wakes up in the morning and thinks, today, I'd like to go mad, lose my job and friends and end up odd-looking and living on the streets, any more than they think, today I'd like to get cancer.

Introduction

Life is not always what it seems: why you should read this book and recommend it to all your friends and family

My aim in writing this book is to shine a bright light into the world of the mind, the brain and our mental health. Whilst much has and is being done in the world of physical health and everyone is aware of the importance of good diet, exercise and rest - the world of mental health is still in its relative infancy, though the advances being made are huge.

Evidence is emerging that not only are our bodies constantly changing, but so are our minds. If, as we are increasingly seeing, not only are our bodies and minds constantly evolving, so we are able to take control and influence how we want the evolution to take shape. Thus we can become slimmer, fatter, more muscular or leaner in body – just as we can become in the mind. Whilst we can, to some extent work within the boundaries of the DNA with which we were born, this should and does not confine our ability to shape our being into whatever form we wish it to take.

My original intention in writing this book was to produce something concise, a bit of a game-changer, a book the reader could not put down till they had finished it cover-to-cover in one read. I had much material to include in this book; though, as a first edition, I have decided to allow this book to focus on the "meat" of my story.

I hope this book appeals and gives you insight. I guess for some it will be life-changing, others just may not get it. However, if it does one thing, that would be to transform the way that mental health and mental illness is perceived. We are both strong and we are fragile. We are both stubborn and we are sensitive. The more we can be kind and compassionate to both ourselves and others, the more wonderful will be the world we live in.

The following was written whilst I was psychotic - that is, I had no cognition - the part of my brain that distinguishes right from wrong had, in effect, "disappeared". Cool, eh?

Written Tuesday 21 June 2011:
1. prioritise what is really important and what is not
2. take some quiet time out to read, walk, think, chill and sleep
3. write down the dream world you want for yourself
4. take one small step towards it
5. exercise
6. get counsel from a friend who will listen and help you
7. look at your eating plan
8. leave your iPhone turned off – enjoy the silence

Chapter 1
The girl and the robot: my psychosis

The girl and the robot - oh gosh, what a song and how major a role it played whilst I was in what I will refer to as my psychosis.

Mr Invincible I became.

It started sometime around the period February/ March 2011. If I had been writing a diary, what delights that could have contained. During this period, I would have probably been able to have been more precise about what was happening in my mind and in my life, but for the time being I guess an estimate will do.

The triggers, and again, oh how I wish I knew about the importance of triggers before all this began; the triggers were not being able to sleep due to over-activity in the brain which was further exacerbated by over-consumption of coffee (l recall at one point l was consuming - daily - eight eight-cup cafetières of coffee).

At the time I was working at a well-known public sector body in what I thought was my dream job. Since my arrival in Australia in 2009, I had wanted to do more on the project management aspect of my skill-base and as I was qualified and had a degree of experience in this field, I felt I would be well-served in further developing my career path in this field. Little did I know it would almost kill me.

The first inkling that something was not quite right was when I reported to my GP that I was having problems sleeping. A sleep study was organised whereby I was "wired up" with monitors from tip to toe, the result of which was a report and a diagnosis of sleep apnea.

However, from what I can recollect of the time, whilst my GP received the report containing the diagnosis, nothing further was done to address this condition. Sleep apnea is where the individual's breathing affects their quality of sleep to such an extent that in extreme cases they stop breathing. This results in the body communicating to the brain that it is being starved of oxygen, which it requires to function, subsequently resulting in the brain sending out signals to the individual to awake to reinstate their breathing.

This pattern can go on through the night, resulting in broken sleep and minimal quantities of the required deep sleep which enable the brain and body to fully restore itself in preparation for the forthcoming day.

In addition to the diagnosis of sleep apnea, my sleep patterns were completely haywire. One of my recollections of the period between the months of February and March 2011 is of speeding my way to work. I also recall on my return home one day falling asleep at the wheel as a result of sheer mental exhaustion. Not handy when you are in the outside lane doing 80 km/h. Thankfully I was woken up as my car drifted into the middle lane and a ute brushing my wing which awoke me and enabled me safely to bring the car under control on the hard shoulder.

As March progressed into April, I found myself unemployed. Well, what actually happened was that I did not pass my probationary period. A completely trumped-up case was made by my manager, the evidence was completely fabricated and, most likely the result of my increasingly evident psychotic behaviour - of which I suspect I had little awareness.

The whole "quick-get-him-out-of-here" episode was a farce. The organisation with whom I was employed had no HR policies or procedures on their intranet or anywhere else; they were basically making it up as they went along. I remember e-mailing HR to ask them if they could direct me to where I could find relevant HR policies on the intranet to which I received the response the policies and procedures follow best practice and are not available on the intranet. Not bad for a public sector body, upholding public sector ethical standards and spending - quite freely and ineffectively – taxpayers' money.

As I found I had time on my hands, I decided in early

April to fly to New Zealand to see a friend who, ironically I thought was not well and could do with some emotional support (how ironic, I say to myself reflecting back on this period.) Booking the flight through those wonderful people at Flight Centre, I flew out with Emirates and back with Virgin Blue - what a contrast that was.

The flight from Melbourne to Auckland was an early start, thus I decided to take three apples in my hand luggage for sustenance en route. I had checked-in online and took my boarding pass. All went well until I got to Passport Control. Now my memory here is a little hazy but from what I can recollect, Passport Control was not happy with some aspect of my check-in printout and they said it had to be stamped by the Emirates check-in desk. So I went back to the Emirates check-in desk and explained to them that Passport Control would not let me through without an Emirates stamp on my boarding pass. They had never heard of this before and were completely bemused by such a suggestion. Somehow, I got the issue sorted and, by the time I got back to Passport Control, a new set of staff had appeared. Was I involved in a wind-up at my own expense? Surely not.

The flight with Emirates went wonderfully well. I am an absolute fan of Emirates. One point to note though, I took a photo of myself before take-off and I look ill. My face is gaunt, I had lost practically all muscle around my cheekbones and my skin colour was pallid beyond recognition.

On landing, we disembarked the plane and then went through customs where all our bags were scanned. Of course, I had forgotten about the apples I had packed to eat during the flight. I was asked to step aside, open my bag and low and behold, I had committed a major breach of New Zealand's bio-security laws. I was escorted over to another table where a burly female customs officer informed me I had committed an offence and she then produced a card and informed me that I had a choice of one of four options. I recall the last one was something like you have the option to appear before a magistrate to present your case. I also recall asking the Customs Officer if she could advise me on the case law regarding the last option. She responded I had a choice and I had to make a decision. I replied that l would prefer to make an informed choice to which l think I received a gruff response. This all happened in April 2011; only in the last six months have I been in touch with the New Zealand Department of Agriculture to ask what the status of the situation is, including a letter indicating my diagnosis of bipolar disorder and asking what further action might be required to close the matter. I received a response to my letter informing me that the information I had provided would be presented to a judge and I have heard nothing since. I can only assume 'case closed'. As it happens, months after I committed my felony, the Australia and New Zealand governments signed an agreement to allow the import of fruit between the two countries, including apples.

The stay in Auckland, as far as I can remember was fun. I seem to have taken loads of photos on my iPhone. I visited the museum and several other iconic venues. I also remember having a conversation with a lady in a secondhand furniture shop and that she offered me her card, noting that she needed someone to manage a small chain of hairdressers and that I should give her a call. How on earth do I get myself into these situations? Reminder – you were manic – end of.

During my time in Auckland, Borders, the bookstore was going into liquidation, so I bought a number of cheap DVDs and books. However as a result of this, when I got to Auckland Airport I was way over my luggage limit and had a lovely series of interactions with the wonderful staff of Virgin Blue (more on this later in the book).

On my return from New Zealand, I had a routine visit to my GP. The visit took place in last April. I recall towards the end of the appointment our conversation went something like:

GP: "You don't seem well, I'm going to prescribe you

lithium."

Me: "Lithium? Does that mean I am going to go to Coles and on passing the battery stand, want to break into a pack and start chewing on a battery?"

GP: "Well, I am still going to give you the prescription and I would like you to come back tomorrow so we can test your blood."

Me: "You can give me the prescription but l see no need for it."

This is, I understand, having read autobiographies of other people who have been through a similar experience with psychosis, a classic response to any suggestion that either they are not well or that they need to take medication - after all, why should they - they feel fantastic!

I returned the following day to see my GP, having not taken the lithium as requested, nor even been to the pharmacist to exchange the script for the medication. My GP asked me if I had and, when I replied, "I said yesterday I see no need for it," allowed me to leave his room and depart into the big wide world - completely out of my mind/ psychotic/ manic/ loopy-loo!

At this point in time I was on Newstart, which is the basic allowance for those who have no other income. This amounts to $600 or thereabouts per fortnight. It is impossible to subsist on this amount. As a result of my lack of money and need to subsist, I sought additional funds by taking possessions that I felt I no longer required to Cash Converters. I also decided to take up being a masseur and bought a massage table. And yes, I was driving my car around whilst psychotic - scary stuff, methinks. You would think driving whilst drunk or on drugs is dangerous; I wonder how safe it is to drive whilst psychotic? And I am sure this not the first time and nor the last time this will have occurred.

So, from my recollection life was chugging along fairly ok. I was getting a paltry amount of money in as a masseur and also money from the gradual relocation of my apartment to Cash Converters. I also had the grand idea of opening a garden centre combined with a café, single-handedly, with no capital and no – well, anything really. I made enquires with banks about loans, began writing up a business plan and making calls to estate agents about local vacant properties which I felt could fit my requirements. What do I think about all this reflecting back? Complete madness, and I laugh and move on.

Somehow I was getting some form of inclination things were not right. Maybe it was because events would happen like builders waving their arms around as I passed by walking my neighbour's dog and listening to "The Girl and the Robot" by Royksopp or some other wonderful tune on my iPod. At this point in time I can think of no other similar examples but I guess there must have been many. Oh, yes and one of the staff at Cash Converters observing that I had been in there so many times he wondered whether I had anything left in my apartment!

And so I went back to seek advice. Same GP practice, different GP. This time the feedback I got was - "Well, you seem ok but just as way of seeking a second opinion I'll make a referral for you to be assessed by a psychiatrist."

This resulted in my appointment with, in my view, one of the most dangerous people on this planet. As is often the case with clinicians, and maybe through no fault of their own, he appeared 25 minutes after the time that our appointment had been scheduled. I was invited in the room - just me and him. I babbled for some 25 minutes and then stopped. At this point he laughed out loud, concluded I demonstrated all the classic symptoms and noted the following:

- no-one would ever employ me in my current mental state,
- if I was to go on anti-depressants I would likely be sectioned; and
- if I was to go on a plane, I would likely decide to

open the plane door mid-flight (guess he was not aware I had flown to New Zealand in this same state and only been caught trying to illegally import three apples – hey-ho)

He gave a prescription for 25 milligrams of seroquel - an anti-psychotic - and then disappeared only to return with a handful of papers which he informed me I should read as they would give me some guidance on my condition and help me get better. To this day, I have no idea where these papers are and this is almost three years later.

This is the resultant report he produced based on that appointment:

"Dated: 16 June 2011

Re: David Clark DOB: XX/XX/XXXX

Referral

Thank you for referring David. As you are aware, he is a 43-year-old British homosexual man living along in private rental accommodation. He is a recipient of Newstart Allowance. He was referred with manic symptoms for assessment and management advice.

History

David described "a rapid re-emergence of the phoenix out of the fire" since late 2010, associated with 15kg weight loss commensurate with increased physical exercise, and mood elevation. He endorsed all symptoms of hypomania on direct questioning. He had aspirations about becoming a philosopher, a life coach and writing a book. There was no delusional derivation to these ideas, but he acknowledged that they might be related to his mood. He felt more introspective, and "self-actualised". He was unable to recall recent secondary consultation advice from GP psych support (Dr Tracie Hicks) to commence an anti-psychotic or significant change which may be impacting on his ability to work. His symptoms seem to have been reducing in severity since their rather abrupt onset. He has not engaged in any risky behaviour or had dangerous ideation during this time.

This episode occurs on the background of depressed mood secondary to a relationship breakdown in May 2010, being bullied at work (in project management) and in the setting of anti-retroviral therapy (including efavirenz) for chronic HIV infection complicated by some opportunistic infections. He sees a psychologist (XXXX), and he is compliant with anti-retroviral therapy. He had possibly abused alcohol and amphetamines in the past but he was reticent to discuss this today. He denied recent illicit drug or alcohol use. There is no family history of mood disorder, and no past history of hypomanic or manic symptoms. His account of his earlier life was characterised by bullying by his father, and of a flamboyant social life, of which I suspect there is an element of retrospective falsification as a result of his elevated mood state. He previously worked in the XXXX in the UK, and after moving to Australia 3 years ago he worked in statewide XXXX services project management, and participated in advising XXXX. He has knowledge of administrative and procedural activities involved in health care, and he had a relationship with a psychiatrist for 7 years.

Mental state examination

David presented as distracted but cooperative with the interview. He was casually dressed, displayed good eye contact (except when speaking to me, at which stage he looked at the walls) and there was mild psychomotor agitation. There was prolixity of speech which was interruptible. His thought stream was increased in tempo, and there was tangentially and ordered flight of ideas. There were grandiose themes of thought content associated with change. There was preoccupation that he had been patronised/ bullied by people previously in his life, and there was an infantalising method of questioning the interviewer. His mood was objectively and subjectively elevated. His affect had some abnormal reactivity, and punctuated by laughter. There was no suicidal or homicidal ideation, and no intention to jeopardise his HIV treatment. His cognition was not tested in order to preserve a therapeutic alliance.

Formulation

In understanding David, there is a past history of depressed mood in the setting of situational precipitants, but no indication of sustained mood disorder. There is an incongruously absent family history of mental illness. It would seem that David is presenting with a first episode of mania (there is objective evidence of psychosis with formal thought disorder) in the setting of antiretroviral treatment, but there is evidence that this is resolving slightly. The primary risks include occupational impairment and deterioration of mental state (particularly if prescribed antidepressants). This deterioration seems aetiologically linked to retroviral treatment; however, I don't have viral load results - if these were elevated it may indicate HIV mania which may progress and indicate more end-stage viral illness. Alcohol and other substances may be playing a minor role in maintaining his symptoms. The predominant barrier to treatment is possible preference for his symptoms. I do not think that efavirenz is contraindicated currently but it would be worthwhile calibrating my opinion with an infection disease physician. and if we consider efavirenz to be contraindicated then this may remove a treatment option for HIV. I think it is important to prioritise the treatment of HIV at this stage.

Diagnosis Axis I - first episode psychosis, Ddx - Mania, as part of Bipolar Axis ll

Deferred Axis lll - HIV Axis lV - Deferred AxisV-GAF50 possibly medication induced (efavirenz)

Affective Disorder

Management
As discussed over the phone today, I have encouraged David to commence 25 mg quetiapine tonight, for which I have provided a prescription as an opportunistic manoeuvre. I have discussed a method of titrating the dose which is rather conservative and aimed at minimising side effects in the hope that this improves his long term compliance, e.g. increasing by 25 mg every week. I have provided psycho-educational material to David and he has agreed for me to review him again shortly which our administrative staff will arrange. I will discuss with David a consultation-liaison psychiatrist at The Alfred to examine the feasibility of me following him up from August at one of our outpatient clinics. I will contact you in the near future to ascertain his HIV load and CD4 count, and to ask you about infectious disease input that has occurred.

Your sincerely,
XXXX
Senior Psychiatry Registrar"

Every time I read this report it fills me with amazement. This report is, I believe, factually inaccurate. Whilst yes, I may not have been completely with it at the time, I have no idea who Dr Tracie Hicks is, the suggestion that I have "possibly abused alcohol and amphetamines" - what does this mean? And for the record I have never taken amphetamines in my life. With reference to "there is no family history of mood disorder", well he obviously did not ask the right questions here as I would have told him all about that aspect of my life and I talk about it later in this book.

And so May moves into June and at this point I am facing eviction from my apartment. I had been successful in delaying this event due the installation of new windows in my apartment which had resulted in significant condensation on the window sills daily and also due to an ongoing problem with flooding of the kitchen. This had been as a result of my being on the top floor of an apartment block with a flat roof which had not had its drainage channels cleared, probably since it had been built in the 1960s.

I went on rental strike as I was fed up with clearing up the water-soaked kitchen surfaces and was able to "get away" with this for a period of time. However, eventually I ended up in Victorian Civil and Administrative Tribunal as a defendant.

I got there early and watched a video explaining how VCAT worked to ensure fairness in procedure and due process. In reality I was treated as an open-and-shut case - pay up or vacate. The Magistrate did not even look at me, as far as I can recall.

And so I ended up in my current residence with someone who has basically saved my life. Without this person, I would probably be homeless, destitute and even possibly dead. The system currently in place to support those people experiencing challenges with their mental health is, in my humble opinion, a disaster.

I finally came out of my psychosis in late September. I remember the moment distinctly, walking down the street in which I live, shaking my head and then reflecting - what on earth has been going on with me over the past few months.

I continued only on Seroquel for the rest of the year and it was only in April the following year when I was prescribed further medication - lithium (a standard approach for those diagnosed with bipolar disorder) and escitalopram (an anti-depressant). This combination put me through hell mentally. I plunged into one of the worst depressions I had ever experienced and it took me three months of sheer agony to regain some form of consciousness. This process at times involved my consuming a whole bottle of vodka daily to escape the pain. And there was no-one, as I spent each day in bed, sometimes considering the imponderable, I felt, that could or would help me.

At this point in time I had given up on doctors. I had stopped seeing my psychologist after an appointment in early 2012 when he asked if I had got back into gainful employment. My head at this point was still a mess. I was gob-smacked that he had asked such a question. I had been attending appointments with him since a year after my arrival in Australia and really questioned the benefit of the sessions I attended in which I was charged $120 for just less than an hour each time and from which I felt I gained little benefit.

The appointments with the first hospital psychiatrist to whom I was referred took the form of 30 minutes every two months. If anyone can remember Kenny Everett, that is who I saw every time I had to sit opposite him and repeat the same story - head pains, exhaustion, what the hell is going on with my head? And the response I got - nothing. No suggestions, no advice, no guidance, no offerings of hope – just, ok well you seem to be travelling ok so we'll see you in two months' time, if you could arrange your next appointment with receptionist on your way out.

Bipolar disorder is considered the second-most severe mental illness. And this is what happens?

Chapter 2
So tell me sir, what is it like to be a loony?

My aims of this book are many but include highlighting the importance of good mental health, the impact of poor mental health on an individual and an opportunity to break some of the stigma attached to mental illness.

But what is it actually like to be actually mentally ill, to be psychotic, to be "mad"? Whilst I gave a flavour in the previous chapter, I thought I might also include some actual further insight by providing some of the postings I made onto my Facebook profile during 2011. For those of a nervous disposition, I should at this point note there in adult humour contained herein; not much but it is there – you have been warned. Enjoy :)

Posting star date Fri 25 Mar 2011
March 25, 2011 at 8:40am
Welcome to my little diary of comings and goings surrounding the establishment of my new adventure. To date I have a new mobile phone for my business, a name, a logo and a bit of blurb which I am developing to explain the rationale for establishing the company and what I hope it can achieve.

Going forward l will be working on my business plan, sorting out a location within which l will be based, an interior which will reflect the business' philosophy and a business model moulded around the needs of clients who may wish to avail themselves of the services I can offer.

I hope you enjoy reading these little snippets and that they provide a bit of a flavour of what lies ahead - happy to respond to any suggestions, ideas, questions you may have. Enjoy Dx,

My recent Palm Reading
April 5, 2011 at 10:38pm
You are a warm person who is affectionate and

emotional. You have a complex emotional pattern. You are a thorough and careful thinker. You like to experiment with new ideas. You do things according to your own rules. You are confident and able to take charge. You have a strong emotional drive and are a great communicator. Next year can be a very good year for you if you take the challenges that await you and be patient with your friends and family.

An e-mail I recently sent to the CEO of Virgin Blue - no reply as yet.
April 6, 2011 at 7:41pm
Via e-mail
Dear Mr Borghetti,
I am writing to inform you that I am deeply disappointed with my experience yesterday in taking flight DJ165. The content below explains the circumstances and I am seeking some form of resolution to the fact that I have had to leave a suitcase of mine in Auckland Airport and am most likely going to have to fly back to New Zealand to collect this case which is currently in storage at a cost of NZ$10. I am not happy with the service Pacific Blue has offered me especially as this was my first time flying with the airline. The following paragraphs detail my experience.

I arrived at the airport in good time and waited in line once staff had established themselves at their respective desks and begun to check passengers in.

However there was some confusion as, whilst a sign had been put up showing Sydney, there was none for Melbourne. A staff member soon noticed this confusion and intervened by swiftly changing the elastic barriers to ensure passengers were better able to direct themselves to the appropriate desk.

On arriving at desk 90, I was greeted by a polite if slightly sleepy staff member. I provided my documents which she took, reviewed and then began entering details into the computer system. There was minimal interaction between myself and the staff member until her head jerked around and she asked if I had boarded a plane from Raratonga. I informed her that I had not and she apologized noting that it was early and that she was not yet fully wake.

I was then asked if I had any luggage to check-in and I informed her that whilst I was aware that my luggage was over the limit for my ticket, I had purchased a ticket which permitted hand baggage and I wondered what options might be available to enable me to take all my luggage with me. I placed my main bag on the sales and she informed me that I would have to pay $60 to check-in the bag and that I would have to go to a different desk to put this into effect.

I then asked her again about options and she repeated that I would have to go to a different desk and pay $60. As I have extensive experience in international travel, I am aware of the options available and found that staff member's attitude unhelpful.

I then went to the appropriate desk to explore options and again was informed that there the only option would be to pay $60 to check in my bag. Jamie smirked when I questioned whether there were options and I commented that I thought it was inappropriate for her to do so; she did not reply. I found her attitude and approach unacceptable and I asked to speak to a supervisor at which point I was introduced to Josephine. She asked me what had happened and then guided me to desk 96 at which we went through check-in again and then she asked me what had happened. I explained the situation and was informed that the only option was to pay $60. Again, I knew that this was not the only option and so found her approach to be unhelpful. Moreover during this conversation, an elderly Indian lady approached the desk panting and on seeing this lady, suggested Jamie might like to assist the lady before dealing with me. She refused, noting that she would deal with me first and then the lady. Given this elderly lady was clearly in distress, 1 found Jamie's response highly inappropriate and repeated to Jamie that she might like to assist the elderly lady in distress and picked up my bags and went to the Priority Assistance desk.

Through further discussion an alternative option was identified, namely that I could put my case into storage and then either arrange for someone to pick it up and arrange for it to be flown over or alternatively that I fly back to Auckland to pick up the case from the airport.

Thankfully the gentleman at the storage counter was top-notch and was able to assist. He was polite, informative and extremely helpful. I felt he had something to offer staff at Virgin Blue working in the airport this morning.

On returning to the check-in desk, I presented my passport and ticket and was checked in. I was offered a seat by the Emergency Exit, which I duly accepted. However, I was still unhappy with the poor customer service I had experienced and asked how I could make a complaint. I was directed to the Virgin Blue website, advised to login in as guest and recommended that would be the easiest way to understand how best to make a complaint. Being a member of the Facebook generation, I am aware there may be alternative options.

In conclusion, it being my first experience of flying with Virgin Blue, I am writing to inform you of the depth of my displeasure with your ground staff , annoyed that I have to pay additional costs to place in storage luggage I could not take on board with me and would welcome your advice on whether you think I am likely to again receive such poor customer service or that this experience was a one off never ever to be repeated/ and financial reimbursement reflecting the fact that I will not have to fly return to Auckland from Melbourne to reclaim my luggage.

I look forward to reading your considered response to the contents of this letter. I am amazed, given where customers are at and the impact the Facebook generation is having that I have had to go through what I have had to go through and have had to write this e-mail to you.

Kind regards,

Dave Clark.

P.S. I used Google on Monday 4 April 2011 at 8.11pm using the search criteria "Pacific Blue" and "complaints" and within 0.36 seconds was informed that there were 7,870 sites containing these words so I suggest you may have an issue you are not effectively addressing.

A note to Emirates April 6, 2011 at 9:08pm
is loving Emirates....

I am sending you this message to ask what options you can offer me as compensation for the erroneous information contained on your website which is misleading and inappropriate.

I flew last Tuesday from Melbourne, Australia to Auckland, New Zealand via Emirates. Prior to taking the flight, I checked in online and was advised that I could proceed straight to the gate via Customs. However this is incorrect. I was stopped at Customs and advised that I would have to return to the Emirates desk to get the printout of my boarding card stamped by the Emirates desk before I could proceed past Customs.

I went to the Emirates desk and they informed me they did not have a stamp. I was issued a boarding pass and had to go through security check AGAIN.

I was informed by a supervisor at Customs that the information contained on the Emirates website is incorrect but that Emirates in unwilling to amend the site to reflect accurately the process.

I experienced significant discomfort having to go

through this process and would be most grateful if Emirates could provide some form of compensation to reflect this.

Kind regards,
XXXX

Email to my managing agents
April 11, 2011 at 7.57pm
XXXX,

I have just woken to find, in my kitchen, that yet again water has leaked onto the work surfaces.

The work surfaces are flooded and the following items soaked:
- a pizza maker
- a slow cooker
- various other items which I had placed on the work surface within the kitchen area.

I have raised the issue of the leaking roof time and time again and XXXX has failed to address this issue. It is now urgent. I am also not happy with the condition of the window frames; again I have raised this issue time and time again but to no avail. I am now at the point of no longer wishing to tolerate this situation. It is 4.26am. I should not have to be sending you this e-mail.

I await a reply as to how XXXX plan to properly manage XXXX or alternatively provide me with accommodation that neither has a leaking roof nor deteriorating window frames. I understand, legally, XXXX has 14 days from the point of being made aware of repairs being required - this timescale has been exceeded by a number of months.

You will recall the numerous e-mails I have sent you. If legal action is the only course, then I guess that is an option.

Kind regards,
Dave.

Airlines sometimes deliver- but not always ;)
April 12, 2011 at 7.13am

Air steward: Hello Sir/ Madam/ Small, Welcome to Average Airlines, What you like to eat today - meat or fish?

Customer - What meat is available?

Air steward - Sausage, mince or horse

Customer – Well, actually I am vegetarian.

Air steward - Sorry Sir, you will have to get off the plane. We do not accept the use of offensive language on this airline.

Customer - May I be allowed to starve and self-flagellate.

Air steward - You may starve - I can fellate you later if you wish.

Customer - And my wife?

Air steward – Sorry, I do not do fish.

Customer – I think you misheard, l asked if my wife be allowed to starve.

Air steward - Sir, we do not allow ladies to starve - they deserve the best and seeing how you are dressed and treating you wife, I think I may advise her of a good dating agency.

Let the universe decide
April 14, 2011 at 12:27am

So I thought it would be nice to help a friend by spending some NZ$ 400 of my own money to purchase a return ticket to Auckland to see if I could provide him with a little support as he tried to make decisions as to the options that lay before him.

Whilst I enjoyed my time in NZ, I am not prepared to be thrown into a washing machine three times in four days whilst visualizing a scene out of a Harry Potter film where they fly around on broomsticks. Life is too short to be treated like shit and I will not tolerate rude behaviour.

Needless to say we all have choices and the decision I

have to make is should I fly back to Auckland to retrieve my suitcase and discuss a potential business partnership or should I stay in Melbourne, get my case flown back and correspond via Skype and e-mail. Choices, choices - now where is that chocolate bar?

Don't forget - politeness costs nothing. April 4, 2011 at 12:39pm is bemused by people that would prefer to engage in dialogue via any channel other than the rather common-sensical telephone conversation - why and why can't we bring back a bit of face-to-face - actually that could be offensive as I am likely to cough very loudly at the slightest provocation. And here endeth today's sermon. Be nice, it doesn't hurt, oh and colour-co-ordinate please when assembling your clothing daily - colour clashes offend both me and other pretentious pseudo fashionistas :)

Get a grip eh :)
April 14, 2011 at 2:40pm
is two-thirds the way through one of the best movies I have ever seen in my lifetime.

Inglorious Basterds, the film, is a credit to its director and all those who were involved in its creation. I think it is a timely reminder that some people should realise that they do not have a hope in hell of achieving what their heart desires and that they should realise that expressing such desires is plainly stupid and a waste of, not just my, but their time too. Oh dear - how sad that some people should think they are so able that they fail time and time again to achieve. Be nice, do not try to be someone or something you are plainly not and do not, ever, offend anyone else in life. Just be pleasant, kind, mindful - the world will be a more pleasant place for all if you acquiesce to these words.

Time for some plain chocolate, a stroke of a fluffy dog, a smoke of a pipe and a slide into a warm bed. Good nite world.

Songs chosen
April 14, 2011 at 10:24pm

is looking forward to Mr G's show tomorrow - the songs currently chosen are:
1. SoS - Abba: relating to the my early years and my parents' marriage
2. Nothing has been proved - Pet Shop Boys (feat Dusty Springfield): from the film Scandal - cried watching that film
3. Enjoy the silence - Depeche Mode: in an ever crazy world, silence is golden
4. Mad World - Tears for Fears: need I say more
5. You've changed - Sia: 'cos I have ;)

My night at the Peel
April 15, 2011 at 9:13pm
is bemused, reflecting on last night, to have been mistaken as straight by a pissed bi- guy who did not want to load up grindr on his iPhone because it would have cost him $2 on Optus pre-pay and the fact that many thought he was straight. The girl throwing up in the ladies toilet sink was class too as were a number of other events including Mr T doing a brilliant rendition of Spinning Around - very funny ;) Good to see quite a few familiar faces too, hope everyone had a good nite Dx

Monday 18 April - Star Date Log - Rock n' Roll
April 18, 2011 at 12:03pm
So today up late, coffee at Husband then to the local Market to walk away with a prescription for lithium (watch out all car batteries - you have been warned), then a visit to the local Library to catch up on Vanity Fair, few trashy mags, Express International and notice a few quirky characters including someone who looked like the lead singer out of Iron Maiden. Then home, chat on the phone with the lovely Ms J about the outrageous note someone put up on the lobby door about loud sex being a distraction from the quite enjoyment of the neighbourhood, a photo session led by my lovely neighbour and my Audi - photos will be posted later this evening, a drive to the dentist for

90 minutes of dental work , a visit to a very cool shop selling futons and then to the car (no parking ticket - thank you City of Philip blah blah and then into town to the gym, a sesh with the free weights a bit of back work and then into the aqua lounge to experience a bit of nob head behaviour caused by two nons going from the sauna into the plunge pool (avoiding the showers and contravening the clearly displayed instructions), and a plonker who seemed to have an opinion about topics as diverse as AFL players being useless apart from the fact that they can run and then he went on to dis his girlfriend "am amazing" few bouts of self-hypnosis in the sauna and dips in the plunge pool and then - well here I am at the mega cool lobby of the gym typing this at a mega cool apple computer located in the wonderful Virgin Active, Bourke Street, Melbourne, Australia - the world.
Luv ya World :)

Morning achievements - Wed 20 April 2011
April 20, 2011 at 2:35am
Today is the first day of the rest of my life. Achievements so far this morning include a visit to the Centrelink Office on High Street, Prahran where I noticed a significant improvement in the atmosphere, aura and ambiance - wow have they changed, a visit to Optus where the staff there was just plain daft but the lady on the phone was fantastic and a moment where I had to inform to parents that if they did not improve their parenting skills they would have to deal into the future with a couple of juvenile delinquents. Time for lunch methinks ;)

How many more postings on the Gillard Government's failing must I write before something happens and Federal Labour implodes
April 21, 2011 at 12:48pm
The more I explore the Centrelink website the worse it becomes - the website is so out of date - it has not been updated for the most part for two years - this is a disgrace

and unacceptable. Gillard may prefer to travel the globe while her public administration burns to the ground but she is failing abysmally. Her Immigration Minister's words too reflect an appalling disregard for humanity - "they have have chosen the wrong minister and the wrong government" - appalling arrogance and a complete lack of empathy with the plight of the dispossessed whatever the circumstances may be. I am appalled.

Regaining control - not there yet but well on my way :)
April 22, 2011 at 11:43pm
Incredible - more clearing and the realisation that I had lost control - I have collected so many leads, plug, electrical nic-nacs - amazing. The realisation that in my desire to be one step ahead, I had lost perspective who I was, am and wanted to be. The journey continues - this is fascinating. I met a guy last night in the Peel - 27 years old - more intelligent than me - had read I Ching, Descartes. and other philosophers, understood the term critical thinking and was getting it on with an 18 year old who was at home at the time with his family" Life goes on - and I am loving it! Dx

Two dips in the plunge and rock on - here we go :)
April 23, 2011 at 8:58am
When you focus you can achieve anything - if you have no focus you will achieve nothing. I managed two dips into the plunge pool at Virgin Active yesterday - only by calming my mind,
imagining myself lying on a sun-kissed beach and walking steadily and slowly into the ice cold water - sometimes I amaze myself that I can achieve above and beyond what I think I am capable of - it seems, however, that 1 can, if I put my mind to it - achieve anything I want - the World is at my feet ;)

E-mail just sent to Practice Manager, XXXX - wot a plonker he has been ,)

May 11, 2011 at 10.02am
Dear Mr XX,
Thank you for your letter referenced above.

I am appalled to have received such a letter and am sending you an e-mail to complain about both its nature and its tone.

If you had done your research, you would have noticed that I am currently recovering from chest infection. I am fully aware of the outstanding balances and considered your letter inconsiderate and basically downright rude.

On joining the practice, I was neither made aware of the charging policies nor complaints Policy.

I am unhappy with a number of aspects regarding the services provided through XXXX and your letter has made me begin to consider whether I wish to continue to 'attend the Clinic. I will be informing my GP of this e-mail and my dissatisfaction with the manner in which I have be dealt with mainly by you. Whilst I understand you are new to the practice - please note some relationships have been in existence for some time and are based on mutual trust and understanding not arrogance and behaviour that is both unprofessional and unnecessary.

Kind regards,
XX

XXXX City Library - politeness costs nothing Dx
May 14, 2011 at 8:30am
I so do not understand passive aggressive behaviour - for example - XXXX Library - in their today - asking if an e-mail I sent had been received - there was apparently a note on my account advising that a repayment plan be agreed - the individual to whom I sent the e-mail did not have the common courtesy to acknowledge the e-mail let alone thank me for providing feedback which may improve the customer experience for other members of said library. Moreover the dude that served what such a

plonker - grumpy as - dude if u don't like people don't work in a library ;)

Amazing what happens when you use the word unprofessional in a conversation - with a librarian - at XXXX Library ;)
May 14, 2011 at 11:21am
Sent from my iPhone
Begin forwarded message;

> From: XXXX
> Date: 13 May 2011 10:10:03 GMNT +10:00
> Subject: Feedback
>
> Dear Mr Clark,
> Your feedback, addressed to Ms XXXX, is important to us and has been forwarded to me for response.
> In your letter you raise a few issues which I would attempt to address below.
> Notices: Our first and final notices are sent out 7 days after an item has become due as a courtesy reminder of outstanding items. You indicate that his annoys you and I am interested to hear why?
> DVD Collection: Our DVD Collection is one of our most heavily used collections and while we have a process in place to clean and repair, we cannot guarantee that each and every disc is cleaned and repaired as they are returned. We thus ask that patrons take care of the items they borrow. Commercial DVD outlets can afford to clean and repair every disc returned as they do not have to process the thousands of items we do per day.
> Loans Policy: The staff member involved had, as a matter of course, given feedback to her Team Leader including the conversation held with you. Apparently after trying to explain the policy to you and understanding that you were unable to pay anything

toward the outstanding amount owed, she offered to place the items on hold for you until you were able to do so. You suggest that only when you later visited the website did you become aware of the policy . All library members are offered the opportunity during registration to read and accept the conditions of membership prior to it being finalised. This includes agreeing to return borrowed items by the due date or pay overdue charges for late returns as determined by the XXXX Council.

Application of policy: We have a large staff component some having many years of experience and others relatively new. We strive to deliver quality service to all our patrons and encourage staff to apply policies and procedures in a consistent manner. There are situations where, under extenuating circumstances, exceptions are made. These are always reported to the team leaders and taken into account when considering improvements.

To accommodate your circumstances. a note has been created on your record suggesting payments in instalments of the outstanding overdue charges. This will allow you to borrow items despite having an amount owing in excess of $10. Instalments are, however due each time you borrow library items.

Thank you for your compliment on self-service at XXXX Service. This improvement has been well-received by the public eliciting much positive feedback. We will shortly roll out an automated return solution which would further allow us to concentrate on customer care and maintenance of our collections.

We are constantly striving to improve our services and always welcome feedback.

I hope you continue to enjoy the services, collections and facilities on offer at XXXX
Library Service.
Best regards,
XXXX

Life is all about choices
May 17, 2011 at 11:42pm
Ok - so thought for the day - this is gonna be fun - life is all about choices. Sometimes we make good choices, sometimes bad, sometimes they lead to fun and frivolity, sometimes to depression and heartache. At the end of the day, they are our choices. We should blame no-one and nothing. They are all our choices. We choose where we live, we choose how much we earn, we choose our friends, we choose how fast we want to live. We choose every minute of every day want we want to do. If not -we have lost control - of our lives. Herewith endeth etc etc.
Have a great day everyone.
Lurv and kisses.
Me x. tee hee ,)

Cash Converters on Chapel St today asserted I had bought fake goods from Myer in Chadstone!
May 25, 2011 at 7:43am
So today was gonna be a busy day and was all on track when my personal trainer called me and asked me where I was - forgot an 11am appointment with him - whoops - then the whole day went a bit intriguing - so am pondering what to do as a result of Cash Converters making the assertion that an iYiYi unit I had purchased from Myer in Chadstone was not actually genuine and that all they could offer me was $50 - I had previously checked-out the unit and ebay gave me a price of $499 - so wondering what I should do? Dx

Trust and self love :) Dx
May 29, 2011 at 4:09am
So today - Trust - What is trust? Who could you trust should trust Who would you trust? Why trust someone if they are not trustworthy? How can you trust you know lies continuously? When is trust appropriate and when is it not? If you cannot trust yourself - why should anyone be expected to trust you? Some people are not self aware that

they are not to be trust - now or into the future - by anyone. Until self love is achieved. they should remain single - alone - and reflect on what they can do, who they are and who they want to be - each and every second - until they achieve self-love;) Dx

Assume nothing - your life will be so much richer as a result ;) Dx
May 30, 2011 at 11:11pm
So today - assumptions - if we want to minimise stress in our life - we have to be clear and what we want, when we want, who we want from or with or by, where we want it, why we want it and how we want it. If we are not CRYSTAL CLEAR about any of these then we are wasting our lives. For example, 1 was walking around on the weekend noticing an amazing number of people in their cars trying to get on with their lives but going nowhere because they were stuck in traffic jams - all day Saturday and all day Sunday - traffic jams - these are the days people have to themselves - why do they get in their cars and then spend their days sitting, stationery, in them - going nowhere for long periods of time - what a waste. Life is all about flowing along your individual journey, meeting people that add value - zest - and fun to your life - not being confronted with people that deplete your energies, are negative about anything and everything, taken an instant dislike to you the moment they lay their eyes on you or do not GET IT ;) Dx

Do not be angry - be happy - each and every second of your life - now and forever ;) Dx
June 1, 2011 at 8:14pm
"I cannot prevent anyone from getting angry, or mad, or frustrated. I can only hope that they'll turn that anger and frustration and madness into something positive, so that two, three, four, five hundred will step forward, so the gay doctors will come out, the gay lawyers, the gay judges, gay bankers, gay architects ... I hope that every professional gay will say

'enough', come forward and tell everybody, wear a sign, let the world know. Maybe that will help. "

Quote from HARVEY MILK
Anyone who knows what they are, who they are etc etc - should no longer have to hide - be out, be proud - go shopping - what the f*** !

The time to be yourself is now – onwards – be happy not angry – others may try to bring you down, they have their own journey. Let them be. Enjoy Dx.

Judgement
June 9, 2011 at 7:48pm
So today is the day I was supposed to get back on track with my rental payment or else risk being evicted from my apartment – legally.

To be honest - and I have thought deeply about this - I am over the apartment in which I currently live. I have had enough.

As a result of my contracting a chest infection, I have been unable to work and have been relying on Centrelink payments to exist. Whilst in the Centrelink building in the recent past, a guy was shot in the stomach by the Federal Police - this resulted in my losing a week out of my life. The guys that helped with try to push start my car - another week lost. So in effect I have lost a fortnight in terms of getting my life back on track.

Whilst my landlord has been kind enough to extend the time period in which I can repay the rent - XXXX - as always obsessed by profit and not humankind - has applied the legal framework and applied to VCAT so the landlord has an eviction notice which he can use to evict me. Apparently I have two weeks notice to move out.

So anyhow what I am getting at is that - the landlord over the last three years and XXXX also has deemed that it is appropriate that I live in an apartment with only one heater and single glazing on all the windows - moreover the fabric in the bathroom and kitchen is in poor repair and there is a hole in the ceiling in the kitchen - so all the landlord cares about is getting rent - not about me or my wellbeing - in effect. If someone else were to view the apartment and saw the mould on the bathroom ceiling due to lack of ventilation and the hole in the kitchen ceiling - the lack of heating etc etc - I wonder.

So 'tis time to move methinks - time to move. My judgement has been made - I am over being treated in such a manner.

Dx

Control - are you in control of your life or have you lost control?
June 15, 2011 at 12:21am
So today is about control.

We are in control of our lives - every second of every day – l think I might have posted on this before - may be I should compare the two entries on my profile - cripes may be I have lost control of what I write on here - whoops - tee hee. Anyhow - control - so why do guys go to the gym - control - they want control - why do some women wear certain clothes which accentuate certain parts of their anatomy - they want to control ;)

Children are - when young - not in control and look to their parents/ guardians relatives for guidance - herewith a problem. Poor or no guidance leads to children growing up with poor judgement and eventually they risk losing control of their lives as a result.

Marketers try control what we buy through their clever use of colour, smell, touch and taste - all the senses - they use to the max to get us to purchase their goods - look at shop windows, at adverts, TV ads - it is all about control - they want us to lose control of our hard earned cash and spend that cash on their goods/ services - whether or not we actually need said goods/ services.

So in conclusion - lose control if you wish - but be aware - be in control of losing control - and then regain it quickly - otherwise you will suffer - and risk suffering for a lifetime" Enjoy life - be happy - peace. Dx.

To be evicted or not to be evicted - that is the question
June 13, 2011 at 4:48pm
Hi XXXX,

Following on from my previous e-mail, I have been unable to raise the cash to pay for the damage that was done to my car by the apartment window replacement men. Unfortunately there are some things in life you can control and some you cannot and raising the cash to pay for the damage in the timescale you required has not been achievable.

So I guess the apartment owner has a choice. Either to allow me more time to pay off the outstanding rent or to evict me.

Option 1: allow me more time to pay off the outstanding rent - I receive payment from Centrelink on Tuesday and this will cover payment to release my car which I can then subsequently market heavily in the local area - as you may recall it is valued at $9,694. Sale of the car will generate sufficient funds to get me back on track and even pay an additional month in advance if that would be acceptable.

Option 2: evict me - I fully accept the landlord has every right to evict. However he should be aware that we (apartment dwellers) are having problems with the new windows. They are generating condensation daily which results in pools of water on the window ledges. I have, daily, to open all the windows to let in fresh air and ventilate the apartment but the condensation is not disappearing. This is, and I suspect will be, an ongoing problem with the new windows - did not happen with the old ones but is happening with the new. So whoever moves in subsequent to me is going to have the same problem - others in the block have similar problems and one of the apartment owners has complained to the window replacement guys about the problem. In addition, there is still a hole in the ceiling in the kitchen area which you can see through. And there is the stain above the kitchen window resulting from the ongoing inundation of rainwater from the blocked roof drain.

In conclusion, as outlined above - I would prefer the landlord choose option 1 but fully accept if he decides to pursue option 2. It would be a pity as I have got to know most the neighbours in this block and several have said it would be sad if I had to move out as we have become real friends. Moreover I am to get involved in the 2011 census collection process for the local area so remaining in the current apartment would be helpful as I am to be the census contact for the area boundaried by Punt Road, Toorak Road, Commercial Road and Murphy Street for which I am to be paid. In addition, I went for a job interview last Tuesday for a job (similar to the one I did at the XXXX in a similar organisation) with an advertised salary of $150,000 p.a. and am waiting to hear back from them.

I would be grateful if you could forward this e-mail to the apartment owner and look forward to his reply.

Kind regards, Dave.

If only... ;)
July 1, 2011 at 7:17am
If only I was normal - I would be a grandad here and now
If only I was normal - I would be happy in my life
If only I was normal - I would be working 9 to 5
If only I was normal - I would be happy with my wife
If only I was normal - I would have a car and a house
If only I was normal - I would be walking the dog tonight
If only I was normal - I would be on my second wife
If only I was normal - my child would have a child
If only I was normal - I would be having an affair
If only I was normal - I would be watching tele in me chair
If only I was normal - I would planning the weekly shop
If only I was normal - I would be sitting in a traffic jam tonight

If only I was normal - I would be thinking what its like

To live a life of freedom - for me for once for life everything you decide say and do will have an impact on someone
July 7, 2011 at 7:20pm
I never thought I would see this - say this - do this - the world is going through so much change - never believe you are doing the right thing - saying the right thing - deciding the right thing - always step back and reflect - how will what I say, what I do, what I decide - be perceived by the world - the universe - if you feel happy then proceed otherwise review and reflect and be mindful that everything you decide, say and do will have an impact on someone, somewhere at some time - that is what life is all about - enjoy your Friday x

I did it my way ;) Dx
July 27, 2011 at 7:57am
And so, after three years of living in my current apartment - this weekend I will be moving out the final odds and sods - has been a wonderful time - the first place I moved into when I moved over here three years ago. However, too much has gone wrong recently - the new windows are a disaster. the noise from the traffic outside is unbearable and - most important of all - the dishwasher no longer works And so time to move on - to a new wonderful world :) Dx

The Law of Cause and Effect can, occasionally, work in ways we may not have expected :)
August 16, 2011 12:25am
A young man had a terrible fall while mountain climbing. Because of the severity of the fall, he suffered a serious concussion. In order to save the young man, the medical personnel on the scene decided to call in a renowned neurologist located some distance away from where the young man lay. The doctor was at first reluctant but out of

compassion he decided to make the trip. He packed his car with the necessary medical supplies and headed south.

Unexpectedly, half way into his drive, a middle-aged man in a leather jacket stopped the car and ordered the doctor out, saying, "Get out. I need the car".

The doctor immediately explained, "You don't know what you are doing. I am a doctor on an emergency call to save a patient." The car jacker did not wait for the doctor to finish and pulled him out of his car. The doctor had no choice but to hitch a ride from strangers. When he finally arrived at the scene of the accident, many hours had passed and the young man had not survived. The medic on the scene was angry with the doctor for being so late and told him so. When the doctor approached the young man, he saw a middle-aged man crying 'My son, my son". The doctor took a look at the middle-aged man and immediately recognised him as the person who had forced him out of his car earlier that day.

The man in the leather jacket was the young man's father. In trying to get to the scene to see his son, he had indirectly caused his son's death.

Be mindful - Our relationship with others is governed by the Law of Cause and Effect, which can occasionally work in the opposite direction to that we would wish. Sometimes, in trying to do the right thing we actually achieve the opposite.

Have a great day and enjoy each and every second :)
Dx

Eckhart Tolle on Karma - is worth a read ;) Dx
August 29, 2011 at 12:15am
Morning All - Hope you had a restful weekend :)

Just received an e-mail about karma from Eckhart Tolle - some of you may have heard of this guy - he is famous for the book the POWER OF NOW and has written a number of other books on a similar subject. Well I have just read through the text below and fully agree with Mr E - it is not a mystery - it is true - our subconscious in constantly our driver in the car that is us - wanna learn more - message me and we can explore :)

The greater part of most people's thinking is involuntary, automatic, and repetitive. It is no more than a kind of mental static and fulfils no real purpose.

Strictly speaking, you don't choose to think, Thinking happens to you. The statement "I think" implies volition. It implies that you have wilfully chosen to think what you think (or that you think in the first place). For most people, this is not yet the case. "I think" is just as false a statement as "I digest" or "I circulate my blood." Digestion happens, circulation happens, thinking happens.

The voice in the head has a life of its own. Most people are at the mercy of that voice; they are possessed by their thinking and its repetitive, unconscious content. This circular, repetitive, incessant thinking is conditioned by the past, and it keeps you trapped in the past.

It is as though you continue to relive the past over and over again. Do you ever wonder why the same problems challenge you throughout your life? Your unconscious mind is re-creating them, but you don't even know it.

The Eastern term for this repetitive cycle is karma. You continually bring to your life experiences that correspond to your thinking. What you reap, you will sow. What you think you will attract. If the contents of your thoughts are locked in past events, you are destined to repeat them. This is karma. And it goes both ways.

We have heard of good karma and bad karma. Bad karma is the experiences we have that are attracted to us by our mind's obsession with all the bad things that have happened to us.

Bad karma not only produces experiences that are undesirable, it is also a life lived in the past, not the present.

Good karma, on the other hand, comes from living in the present moment. When we liberate our mind from thoughts of the past and negative rumination, we are free to engage our mind in original, creative thought. We are free to be spontaneous and fun-loving. We are free to live our life now with a sense of curiosity, discovery and adventure. Far from being trapped in a cycle of negativity, we live a life of freshness, proactivity and healthy self-expression.

If you have been living life in the past, caught in the cycle of bad karma, you can get free of it.

Just in the way that thinking happens to you, bad karma happens to you. It is an involuntary predicament. It is a condition that you do not consciously choose.

The solution is to begin choosing what you want for yourself. Instead of being a victim of your own thinking, be an active, engaged choice maker.

- Choose to be more present.
- Choose to be more aware of what thoughts are circulating in your mind.
- Choose to engage your mind in original, creative thinking.
- Choose to make your mind an interesting, adventurous place.
- Chose to make good karma by using your mind for positive and productive thinking.

Chapter 3

The warning signs - if only someone had told me

My childhood was pretty idyllic, I guess. From early childhood up to the age of ten, I lived in a village called Helpston. Helpston also happens to be the birthplace of John Clare (I included a sample of his poetry early on in this tome), who ironically, experienced symptoms similar to mine – during his lifetime the condition was labelled manic depression. Sadly his path took a rather different route to mine and he was admitted and subsequently died in a mental health institution.

I lived opposite a cemetery with Mum and Dad in a house that Dad had built, as far as I know single-handedly and in front of a farm. I use the word idyllic as, from my recollection, it was. School was great fun and, despite my parents dissatisfaction with the quality of teaching - I enjoyed getting involved in various activities, was good at athletics and also got involved in the school plays, one year playing Tiny Tim in Christmas Carol and the following year playing Captain Hook in the school's portrayal of Peter Pan. Nothing out of the ordinary there.

My father decided for some reason that he needed to be nearer into town and in 1978 we moved to the suburb of Werrington, what I refer to as my teenage years. Whilst the relationship I had with my father in my early years was, from what I can recollect, pretty ordinary, in my teenage years it was appalling.

The house move was at one of the most challenging times in a child's development, the transition from primary to secondary school - around the age of 10/11 - just as they are entering the wonderful phase of teenage-hood. I began a new primary school six months before the end of the last year in primary school, was found to be somewhat behind in my schooling and was given two key roles in the school

- neither of which I can recall I asked for but somehow attained - that of joint bell ringer marking the start of the school day and the start of and end of morning and afternoon breaks (this was a role treasured by some as it was seen as a position of power!) and the worst crime of all - town-crier at the Mayday school celebrations. I was an outsider as I had arrived in the last school year and considered something not short of a pariah as I had taken not just one but two of the most coveted roles at the school. Ouch!

And so to secondary school, the school I would have gone to even if I had stayed at my old primary school - oh the joy and politics of catchment areas. If only politicians and people in power knew the angst such issues cause families and children as they get out their maps and their pencils and draw those arbitrary lines.

Secondary school was one of those dual existences. You enjoy some bits but not others, some subjects are interesting, some boring. Some teachers are really good at what they do and some should really go explore another craft. And so as time progresses I was streamed into the A grade at the age of 13 and continued in the same stream throughout my schooling. At the age of 14 we were required to make choices regarding what subjects we wished to pursue to examination stage. I was no good at chemistry and the biology teacher was hopeless and I found the subject really dull so they were out, as were woodwork and metalwork; too hard. I did, however, enjoy languages and geography - especially social geography and so my choices were fairly easy to make.

It was around this time or just before that I had my first major mental health breakdown, I guess. My parents and I were on a trip to Whipsnade Zoo; Father (notice change in language) had parked the car and we were walking towards the entrance. I cannot recollect what was being discussed but I can remember quite clearly that I began to walk faster than my parents. I gained such a pace that for a while I was quite a distance from them. I took a circuitous route back to the car park for some reason. What I had not become aware of was that my parents had been rapidly advancing on me and suddenly I experienced a series of punches from my father, my next recollection is of being pushed into the car followed by further punches. A couple of families were in the car park and noticed this happening. The two fathers protested to which my father replied, "Mind your own business, you know nothing." I recall crying the whole journey back and a few days later, whilst my parents were away, taking down the loft ladder and planning the easiest way to hang myself. I even recall going to the extent of putting the "rope" around my neck. Thankfully I took it no further. I was, however a complete mess mentally.

There were subsequent altercations with my father through my teenage years. A combination of my teenage development, I guess and his ever-random mood swings. It became routine to check-in with Mum to see if my father was in a good mood or not. The slightest thing could set him off - his temper was like a volcano eruption. There would be many times during my teenage years when we would not speak and poor Mum would have to be the go-between, even whilst we were in the same room. How she tolerated it I do not know, but she did. And so the teenage years progressed. I was 12 when Margaret Thatcher was elected Prime Minister and became fascinated whenever she appeared on TV. This was a new era. From being a collector of newspapers for recycling at my former primary school, I progressed to a newspaper delivery boy. Round No. 1 I had, notice a pattern emerging here? The round covered one of the first large new estates in Werrington and I loved the job. Two things I was doing at this time that have impacted me since however: I used to listen to music on my Walkman whilst perhaps the volume was a little louder that it should have been and now my hearing is a bit ropey in loud venues and, I guess as a result of carrying large bags full of newspapers, I have mild scoliosis in my spine.

Note to teenagers everywhere - look after your health - or it will bite you on the bum in later life!

And so as time progressed, so did my journey towards the dreaded exams. I took 8 'O' levels at the age of 16 and I guess got not-bad grades – cripes, in writing this I can't even remember the exact number of A's, B's and C's. The biggest challenge at this time, apart from the stress of revising for so many different subjects, was the fact that my supportive father decided it would be a good idea to go on holiday to Westward Ho for a week's break, the week before exams were due to start. And so I had to pack all my revision notes and study whilst supposedly on holiday. Helpful? NOT!

And so whilst I did well at my '0' levels, I completely bombed in my 'A' levels - C and two D's - I was officially in dunce class as far as I was concerned. The two B's and one C I had been predicted to achieve by my teachers seemed a distant dream as did the places I had been offered at Warwick University and Keele University, Kent was also in the mix but maybe I did not get offered a place there. And so my destination was Portsmouth Polytechnic - I was heading south. A three-year experience studying for a degree in Economics, a subject I knew diddly squat about but was reassured a good degree was completely attainable in the timeframe allotted.

I had had a challenging time at secondary school. Whilst I had enjoyed the experience overall, I was frequently bullied and often did not feel part of the whole school life. But then again I had three brilliant friends with whom I had first developed friendships at primary school and with whom I remained friends throughout my teenage years.

The transition to polytechnic, or as it is now known "Portsmouth University" was, for me, a very challenging experience. I guess in a way I disappeared into a kind of shell.

Why? Because I was increasingly grappling with my self-worth, something my father had it seemed been on a campaign to belittle. Moreover I was also battling with my sexuality. I knew what I felt in my heart but my brain did not like it. I was in continuous internal conflict.

And so I played it small. Not very social. Scared of going out. Added to which, Portsmouth was a navy town. The locals did not really get on with the navy bunch but they truly loathed the student population. The navy bunch loathed the students and the students, well, they just had to get on with life and I guess, in one way or another they did and still do as Portsmouth University has expanded to now occupy much of the town centre.

The first year of my degree was pretty much an introduction into economics, all fairly basic and standard with exams at the end of each year and coursework. The second and third year consisted of set topics and options to be chosen from. The first year was pretty uneventful. I lived on campus in a tall tower block on the edge of Portsea Island, on which Portsmouth is located. The tower block was in a rather exposed location and when the wind was strong you could feel the building sway as the wind howled around the concrete structure. Kinda cool when you are dragging your tired mind through a book with the enthralling title of "Introduction to Microeconomics".

One event that I guess is worth a mention: whilst myself and three other friends were walking home one evening back to our "Halls of Residence", we decided to take a shortcut along a pathway behind a long row of terraced houses. We were approached from behind and whacked with what I can best describe as planks of wood. I cannot remember much more about the incident. Our attackers ran off, I guess they must have marked us out as students and this was their way of saying 'we are not happy so we are going to whack you'. Weird that whilst I type this I can feel a slight tingling in the place I was whacked some 25 years ago. Strange but true.

Alcohol played a fairly large part of student life, especially in the first year in halls. Prior to my arrival in Portsmouth, I guess I had had a fairly run-of-the-mill relationship with the stuff. Introduced at a fairly early age by my wonderful mother, she used brandy to settle upset tummies – and gosh did I have a weak digestion system in those early days – was my one of my mother's most successful parenting strategies in my view. As I grew up as a teenager I was allowed the occasional shandy – lemonade mixed with either beer or lager. Then when reaching seventeen and eighteen down the pub Friday – how Mathematics on Friday afternoon seemed to be so much more enjoyable with a couple of pints of the landlord's best inside you. Dozing off was the biggest challenge, made worse by the fact that me and the gang all sat in the front row!

My parting gift on passing my A levels was to try my hand at home brewing. I decided to get the kit to make some white wine – can't recall what genre. Set it all up, follow the instructions to the letter and waited for the bubbles to emerge. And waited. And waited. So after a few days past the allotted time period when the bubbles were supposed to appear I began to add sugar to try and speed up the fermenting process. By the time it did start to bubble after a few days it was producing more bubbles than a jacuzzi on full speed. I decanted some of this wonderful brew into a cordial bottle and I and "the gang" went down to the local for a couple of pints in the beer garden. And then to the homemade wine – it must have been well over 20%! We got plastered.

On arrival in Portsmouth, my introduction to the big wide world began. And for students, freedom, and along with this the opportunity to consume large quantities of alcohol went hand in hand. This was the golden age of the late 1980's, basking in the glow of the Thatcher boom. And it was also the age of the snakebite – a mixture of cider and lager. And if you wanted to take it to the next level: snakebite black – a mix of cider, lager and blackcurrant!?! I tried it and could not stand it. But there seemed to be kudos in consuming up to 8 pints of this mixture in one evening. And some would boast that their consumption across the week amounted to up to 50 pints of this stuff. Wonder how they are now?

It is funny what challenges you face in a new environment. Some pretty predictable, which can be planned for and other come completely out of the blue. One such challenge I faced was how to use a washing machine. Eighteen years old and I had absolutely no idea where to start. Confronted with a top loader, I had no idea about washing powder, conditioner or which buttons to press, washing cycles, the importance of temperatures and checking clothing labels – nothing. Mum laughed her socks off when I had to make the call and confess I had a minor emergency on my hands.

And so to my second year as a student. Due to limitations in student accommodation, the majority of students had to find their own accommodation after their first year and there was a plentiful supply across the island. However, whilst I had a motley crew with whom to share, we were not best organised and were rather late in resolving where to live, as a result of which our abode for our second year was to be in the north of the island - cheaper rent but a bit of a trek from our campus.

The second year? Well, to be honest, I cannot not remember much. This is fascinating from a number of perspectives. I really question all the effort placed on education in the early years and when I say early years – I mean from the beginning of schooling pretty much to the end of finishing my degree – I have used very little of what I learnt during these years in my subsequent career and life. However there is so much time, money and importance attached to these years. For what purpose? Grades? Stereotypes? Classifications? Surely the primary purpose should be to facilitate the journey towards success and enabling each individual to empower themselves to fulfil their dreams – whatever shape they may take, what direction they may wish to follow – to maximise the potential of each one to live the life they want to live?

In my third year, I choose to do Accounting and

Finance, International Economics, Social Economic and Managerial Economics. I choose to focus my dissertation on the UK IT Industry. And I had my first major brain snap.

It is such a wonderful term - brain snap. I had not heard the phrase whilst in the UK but it is often used in Australia. It also describes quite neatly what I was experiencing. A bit like when an elastic band is stretched to a point beyond which it can no longer function, it snaps. And so with the brain. A brain snap results in an outburst of language and usually anger, often unexpected and unwarranted - short in length and deep in intensity. The context? We were, some dozen students, waiting for the Managerial Economics lecturer to appear to lead an hour long seminar. My recollection is that he was just over 20 minutes late when he appeared. There was an exchange between us and I subsequently left the room. I can recall I had felt a growing frustration prior to his appearance about his tardiness but I did not expect nor plan the outburst - that was spontaneous. I did subsequently apologise to him but I consider that the event resulted in my achieving a 2.2 rather than the treasured 2.1 which I had been en route to achieving. Again my brain, a blessing and a curse.

I was not really sure what I wanted to do after graduation. My father gave me a choice before I started my degree - either I was to be a doctor, an accountant or a banker "as you never see any of those people out of work". His original expectation was that I go immediately from school into work and because I did not, he determined that once I began my degree, I should pay rent at home as well as when away.

As I was doing a degree in Economics, and I felt accountancy was not quite me, I tried to find a middle ground which could minimise the grief I might experience from an over-bearing father and could maximise the joy of providing a career path with opportunity and interest. I applied to the then Big Four accountancy firms and also to the National Audit Office. Whilst at the same time as completing my degree, the thoughts of travel began to emerge. A friend was planning to travel round the world and the thought of such a prospect seemed rather appealing. As time progressed so did applications and interviews. A first interview at the National Audit Office was followed by a second interview which resulted in a job offer. In this process, I noted that I was considering travelling round the world as a result of which they concluded that I had a wish to have a year off and then begin my career, an option which was on offer. However, in the meantime my fellow traveller had become ensconced in his first "meaningful" relationship and concluded that he no longer wished to go travelling round the world. Oh the joys of life. And so I found the decision for myself made – I was to travel round the world - single-handedly - with little knowledge of what, where, who or how. Thankfully as time progressed this would all be resolved but at the time I thought.... what the X*&^%$ do I do now?

As you can perhaps imagine, dealing with a father whose view is that university is a waste of time had very little understanding of why anyone should want to go travelling - anywhere - and round the world - get yourself a job and a career! Well I had that sorted, kinda, so all I had to do was sort out the gap year; I fell on my feet. This was the time of Sky TV and it was just being established in the UK. I was seeking temp jobs and News International were seeking out people to help them with this new thing called satellite television. It was a dream come true. I was in from the start and involved from the early marketing campaign through the establishment of regular subscribers and then to a more formalised set-up and became a team leader at the tender age of twenty - I had six in my team - we were one of the final teams dealing with processing applications and we got the job done with a laugh and a smile!

I could not have asked for a more perfect opportunity. A chance to develop my administrative skills, my team skills and my management skills. It got to the point where some of us were working seven days a week, 10-hour days and weekends and loving it. Our work lives were our social lives, we all got on, loved the work and so it went on.

By the time my six months were up it was time to set off on my grand trip. I had a fairly healthy financial reserve on which to draw. I was also pretty lucky in that another temp who had joined the crew some three months in was also planning to do a round-the-world trip and so we teamed up and away we went.

The trip we planned - in the context that the amount I knew about the world you could have written on the back of a postage stamp - London to Bangkok overland to Singapore then fly to Cairns overland to Sydney then to Auckland then to Honolulu then overland to New York flying back to London.

We took off on 21 January 1990. I remember the build-up had been so busy with preparations and with work that it was only when I was sat in the plane looking out the window onto the tarmac did the full scale of what was about to happen finally sink in. An immense wave of trepidation and excitement swept over me - summed up neatly by the phrase, "Oh heck!"

I wrote a diary every day for six months. I hope I still have it somewhere, it would make a cracking read and maybe I might even publish that too. After all, it changed my life. This was a time when backpackers were becoming more prevalent though not an overwhelming breed. I am not sure where things are at now but back then there was a kind of innocence about the whole thing. The fun of meeting people in New Zealand who you had last seen in Singapore or meeting people in Thailand and on departing shouting out, "see you in Oz in two months' time!"

Getting off the plane in Thailand was an experience. Previous destinations had included the Isle of Wight, Isle of Man, the Channel Islands and Austria! My parents were not big on travel. I did venture to Belgium, though only

Ostend, as the first holiday without my parents but with a school friend - we were both eighteen. So Thailand was truly "pushing the envelope". On disembarking the plane, we were met with a wall of heat and humidity. Phew, it was hot!

We were extremely lucky. Our travels were full of fun and minimal drama. Thailand is a country of extremes. Whilst I enjoyed Bangkok, the best part of the country, I felt was further north, in and around Chang Mai. Both myself and my travelling companion experienced the joy of "digestion-disruption" during our journey but he got it real bad early on and was bed-ridden for a number of days. Thankfully he managed to recover and we were able to go on a four-day hill-trek into the mountains. A group of about ten of us set off and travelled through various villages, meeting with tribes and local folk and eating and sleeping at pre-arranged destinations. Two highlights were a ride along a river on a bamboo raft, made particularly awesome in the clear blue sky and gently warming sun and a ride on an elephant with an unexpected shower thrown in for free by the elephant in front of us who decided we needed a wash.

The rest of the journey was pretty fun. Travelled overland down the west coast of Malaysia, through places like Melaka and Kuala Lumpur through to Singapore. It was such a culture shock to arrive in Singapore after a month passing through both Thailand and Malaysia - the oddest experience I can recall was travelling on an escalator - it just felt weird!

Australia was, and still is, awesome. We flew into Cairns and this is where my travel partner and I parted ways. He was a little more attracted to the "booze and the birds" whereas I was, by this point, fast running out of money and the money was in Melbourne - or so everyone told me - there's gold to be had down there and it's in the form of temporary work and lots of it!

And so on a Greyhound I embarked, travelling across and down through inner Oz to the delights of Alice

Springs and the most awesome Uluru (then better known as Ayers Rock).

Another memorable moment - swimming in the pool at one of the cheaper residences, doing backstroke and looking up into the night sky and seeing stars sparkling in the deep dark blue sky. Such an amazing feeling of space and peace – awesome.

From central Oz down to Adelaide where I had my first taster of what was happening back in the UK. I was sitting in a café and they had the TV on in the background and there, for all to see, the Poll Tax Riots. I was gobsmacked. What on earth was happening! It did seem kinda scary but hey I was halfway round the world and life had to go on and go on it did.

From Adelaide to Melbourne - woot woot - my home town. I ended up living here for three of the six months I was on the road, living in a backpackers for those staying longer-term. It was basically two houses which had had rooms converted with three bunks beds in each - how much money was that landlord making?!!!

This period was such a laugh. I got a job delivering internal mail at the main city council. This consisted of three runs around two buildings and the various departments therein. There were a few challenges including remembering which department was where and trying to direct mail that had been addressed Bob Green with no other details - eventually you got to know who lived where, gradually each round became routine. I started at 8am, each round took an hour and I finished at 4pm. I got paid A$12 an hour. I was very grateful.

Sadly I had to move on and a visit to Canberra was followed by Sydney then the east coast and the delights of places including Byron Bay and Noosa Heads, oh yes, and the state capital of Brisbane. I love Canberra, one of the most amazing spectacles is walking between a couple of the buildings and before you emerges the delights of Capital Hill and the new Parliament House in all its majesty. There is one thing that Australia, I feel excels at and that is architecture.

New Zealand was spectacular as it always is. I travelled round the north and the south islands tagging along with three others - great fun it was - we were part of a group on an old coach, staying at various venues and sightseeing at various stop off points. By this time winter had set in so there was a bucket and a half of snow around on the south island which meant the opportunity to try out skiing for the first time. Well, the first day was ok, but as the day progressed with the sun out, the snow had melted, overnight froze and was then covered by a fresh layer of snow in early morning. So by the time we got there it was hazard time. I was ok on the upper slopes but by the time I got two-thirds down, over I went skiis-akimbo - not a pretty sight. Still, no bones broken - though the likelihood of my being so brave on the slopes again, that dream had vamoushed.

Honolulu was hot. I did the pommie classic and as soon as I had landed, checked-in to my accommodation and connected with a couple of other fellow travellers, we headed to the beach. Sadly I forgot to put on any sunscreen. Stupid boy! For the first time in my life, I burnt the inside of my ears and my eyelids - lesson learnt.

There was not much time left on the plane ticket and money was limited too. And of course, I had to get across America, overland. Hey ho, all good. And so to Los Angeles where I was lucky enough to be met by the parents of a fellow backpacker I had met in Thailand - what a wonderful world and what wonderful people they were. They put me up and showed me around the highlights. Universal Studios, Hollywood Hills, Beverley Hills - the works. So wonderful.

And then the joyous ride across America. I embarked on my cross-country Greyhound trip on Tuesday early morning, changed buses in Texas on Thursday and arrived in New York early Friday morning. My flight was due to take off that evening. So imagine my delight when I got off the coach to find my rucksack not there. Did I have kittens?? Apparently my bag had failed to change coaches with me and had decided to rest awhile in Texas before taking a later coach. Thankfully it arrived in time for me to get to JFK airport and the plane home. I landed back in England on 21 July 2000, exactly six months after I had taken off.

So I had achieved a major milestone. I had travelled round the world. And I had travelled halfway round the world on my own! How proud was I. Despite all the attempts of my father to diminish my self-confidence and self-worth, I had achieved. I could achieve. I was an achiever.

However this self-confidence soon dissipated as I whiled away the time before I commenced my job in London in late August of that year. It took a matter of weeks between July and August for me to feel slowly deflated to the point I felt almost worthless. All that progress - gone. But not forever.

I have written a lot about my round the world trip because it meant a lot to me. It shows that life is full of opportunities. And when we are at our lowest, we can always look up at the stars in the knowledge that our dreams are up there with them and awaiting our arrival, their brightness beckoning us towards them. Our brains, our minds are wonderful things but they are delicate. We are not told this, either by our parents, our relatives, our teachers, anyone. I will return to this later in the book. We are the captains of our ships and each one of us can achieve our full potential if we just take care of what we are given along the way.

My career at the National Audit Office was, for me, a once-in-a-lifetime experience for which I will be eternally grateful to all those who gave me opportunities. From the lowly Assistant Auditor who spent the first four or so months reading the newspaper because "there was no work to do", rising through the ranks to Auditor then failing my final accountancy exams, I think five times, to finally qualifying and becoming a Senior Auditor. On qualifying,

I moved from financial audit to value for money audit. Whilst I enjoyed working in the different bodies, I was involved with auditing, I did not like financial audit - not my thing.

By this point, I had worked with a number of teams on different value for money studies. My first on Accident and Emergency Departments in England, then Clinical Audit in Scotland followed by Clinical Audit in England. These reports offered me an excellent introduction into the art and science of value for money and all those involved were and are still masters of their craft. Thank you Jane and Aileen!

My first full report was a real "thrown in at the deep end" task. The initial research had already been carried out but as a result of a personality conflict, the individual possessing all the research (mostly in their head) resigned and took most of the intellectual capital underpinning the rationale for the report with them. And so it was left for me to pick up the pieces of the study which when finally published on 10 June 1999 took on the humble title of "The Management of Medical Equipment in NHS Acute Trusts in England". It was a report bigger than Ben Hur. It was up to me to rescue it. The manager of the team was on secondment from the Audit Commission to learn how we did our value for money work and I still had my "L" plates on and felt very much the novice in terms of what was required to complete such work. So I had to effectively manage the fieldwork, which included site visits to eight hospitals and a national survey of all NHS acute trusts (I think over 200 at the time). The workload was immense, including writing up interviews, completion of audit programmes and production of audit reports to be submitted to each hospital trust visited. It was a challenge, but then again, I guess you learn through experience!

The report I was involved in after that was much more enjoyable - "Hip replacements: Getting it right first time", published on 19 April 2000. It was one of the times in life, again when you are working with a master of their craft but you are also able to have fun. These key ingredients result in you being so energised and motivated that you find work to be a complete pleasure. And so it should be. One of the more memorable moments on this study was when we had our first meeting with a consultant surgeon and my manager, who was leading the interview, mentioned a number of times his fascination with the hip replacement. Whilst I quietly sat and took notes, I kept saying to myself, no, it is the hip prosthesis you are interested in please (call it intuition but I could see what was about to happen!). So of course by the fourth time of mentioning this, the surgeon said – well, I have a patient I am operating on in an hour or so, if she consents you can come in and watch! And thus, an hour or so later, we were gowned up and guided into the operating theatre where a rather large lady lay, fully anaesthetised on the operating table ready to have her life transformed (it is widely considered that hip replacement surgery is one of the most beneficial operations available in terms of improvement to quality of life; it also has one of the longest waiting lists). I am not good with blood, well ok with small quantities but this was pushing it a little. I did almost pass out, I think just after the surgeon invited us to look at his completed masterpiece - ball inserted into hip joint and prosthesis inserted into the hollow bone of the thigh. One of the most rewarding aspects of my work with the NAO is that it had some effect:

"The Independent dated 19/ 04 /00
Questions all patients should ask of surgeons
A list of 19 questions patients should ask before having surgery to ensure they get the best treatment is proposed today by the head of the National Audit Office, the independent watchdog on government spending.

Sir John Bourn includes the list in a report on

hip replacements that exposes wide variations in the care provided to patients in different parts of the country, Sir John found evidence of discrimination against patients who were excluded from surgery on the grounds of their age or weight.

The questions cover the surgeon's success rate, the risks, for how the surgery is likely to be effective and what other options there are. With slight adaptation, it could be used for any operation.

An investigation by the audit office found one in 12 consultants imposes an upper age limit for new hips of 90 to 95 - despite the fact that the Queen Mother, who is 100 this year, has had both hips successfully replaced in the past five years.

One in three consultants refuses surgery to people who are overweight, on the basis that a new hip would not last. However, the weight limit imposed by different consultants varies widely, from 14 stone to 20 stone. The report says: 'This calls into question the equity with which patients are considered for surgery and implies that in some cases whether or not a patient is offered surgery depends on which consultant he or she sees.'

About 8 million people suffer hip pain, usually cause by arthritis, and the NHS does more than 30,000 hip replacements a year at a cost of £139m. The report says it is 'a highly effective procedure, producing immediate and dramatic benefit in almost all cases'. However, between 10 and 20 per cent of patients suffer complications, including infection and loosening of the joint, which may require a repeat operation. These are more complex, more expensive and less successful.

The best chance of success lies with an experienced surgeon but the report found 71 per cent of consultants performed fewer than 10 repeat operations a year and one in 12 performed fewer than 10 initial operations. 'This may be insufficient to ensure outcomes are maximised,' says the report, 'Hip replacements: Getting it right first time'.

Fewer than half of consultants monitor the success of their work by checking the rate of re-operation, the incidence of infection or the proportion of patients free from pain. The report says this is a matter of concern and warns that, without monitoring, problems may not be picked up.

An example of what can go wrong involved the 3M Capital hip used between 1991 and 1997 in 4,744 patients. It turned out to have a failure rate as high as 20 per cent and in 1998 the Department of Health issued a hazard warning and all patients were recalled for checks.

More than 60 artificial hips are in use, costing between £300 and £2,000. The choice of device rests with the individual surgeon but the original design introduced by John Charley in the 1960s has proved difficult to improve upon.

Under new guidance to NHS trusts published last week, the National Institute of Clinical Excellence said only those shown to last at least 10 years with a failure rate of no more than 10 per cent should in future be used. Newer devices should be used only as part of a clinical trial. The ruling is expected to reduce by more than half the number of devices used."

A spin-off of my work on the hip replacement study was a

personal recommendation to join the Value for Money Development Team, the team that was responsible for providing training and guidance on value for money work and also on provision of advice and reports to senior management on various aspects of value for money work. I joined the team bushy-eyed and bright-tailed and full of a mix of emotions ranging from excitement to feeling mildly petrified of the role I was taking on.

However as time progressed, I worked hard, built up my confidence, knowledge and skills sufficiently to demonstrate that not only was I able to fulfil my role but also that I could initiate more innovate approaches allowing the rest of the team to get on with their work whilst I was able to quite ably work under my own initiative. This resulted in my playing a more significant role in the team, taking on the role of lead trainer and as a result of which I ended up providing training to both internal staff but also to audit offices of countries wishing to join the European Union. This resulted in travels to Estonia (twice, Bulgaria, Romania, Hungary, Turkey and the Turkish Republic of Northern Cyprus. The icing on this cake was working with the Accounts Chamber of the Russian Federation. We travelled out there three times and the team we were working with visited us, I think twice. The project was a complete success and I understand the resultant work was considered "the gold standard against which all future reports would be judged". Gulp. So all was good. Apart from one minor but rather significant episode: another brain snap. In fact I had two in my training role. The first was in a meeting with my boss's boss and his boss. What a time to have such a thing happen eh? Still until you understand, you just accept and go... WTF! We were meeting to discuss a paper I had written on a new training programme for value for money staff - it would result in a complete overhaul of the way we did training - it was massive. I sat quietly as these two senior gurus sat and discussed the contents of the papers. But again the same symptoms, I could feel rising up within me. And then the outburst - "what about cost? There is nothing in the paper about cost". Where did that come from eh? Why should I care? Why was it an issue? Who knows, it happened, move on - line through promotion, next please. So that was the third brain snap, occurring in my early thirties and then the next one happened in, of all places, Moscow's second airport. We had just completed another successful week of training and all had gone well. But I was exhausted. We got to the check-in desk. There was a problem with the visa on my passport. The name on the visa did not match the name on my passport - a typo. I exploded. My poor colleague was beside himself but to all his credit he managed to both manage me and the Russian Airport Authorities and eventually we were homeward bound. Not a pleasant experience though, for either him or me.

Another intriguing aspect of my journey to date had been I guess a high degree of restlessness. This was a challenge I could not understand during the time I lived in London. I found it very difficult to sit at home and relax. I always had to be out doing something or going somewhere. This may have been a contributing factor to my desire for travel and the need to explore. As I have already mentioned, I went with work to a number of countries across the European continent. Other countries whose capitals I have visited include:
- France
- Germany
- Netherlands
- Sweden
- Denmark
- Finland
- Italy
- Spain
- Portugal
- Switzerland

And so to the warning signs - well, they were all there. Hyperactive mind, restlessness, need to achieve, parental behavioural abnormalities (I feel fairly sure my father and his mother had symptoms of undiagnosed bipolar disorder - there are family tales that my father's mother used to discipline him by grabbing his hand and pushing it into the fire or alternatively throwing him down the stairs), brain snaps due to over-exertion of brain functioning. Bipolar disorder is considered a mood disorder in that it is the result of a chemical imbalance in the brain. This means that most of the time it is able to function normally. However, depending on the degree to which there is a chemical imbalance, the brain - once whacked out of kilter, is unable to function normally and in effect is unable to self-regulate resulting in over or under- processing of information labelled often as mania and depression.

We all have a brain but so few of us truly understand both the magnificent opportunities it can bring us and also the grave dangers we may face should we not look after it carefully. It is well acknowledged now that our brains are constantly evolving, rewiring itself, re-organising, storing and re-processing information in order to help guide us through our lives in the best way it can.

It is a jigsaw that, once you have all or even some of the pieces, can help you understand who you are and what you can be. I should take this opportunity to note that there is what is called a predisposition to mental illness. This is where signs arise that, if picked up early, can enable the individual to minimise the impact on their journey. However there seems to be minimal awareness of these signs amongst doctors on the frontline. My message to you is – look into the eyes of those you love and care for. If you see warmth and connection, then all is good. If you see distance and paleness, consider seeking additional advice from a medical expert.

Chapter 4
The system is stuffed -you have to take control even when you are not in control

Unless you have had direct experience of the health system, I guess you will have little understanding of how it functions, how it can deliver amazing results and how it too frequently fails those at their most vulnerable.

I guess it is kind of ironic that after having spent some twenty or so years examining the effectiveness of various aspects of UK and Australian health systems and training others to examine the effectiveness of their own healthcare systems, it would soon be time for me to see the other side of the fence and become a service user myself.

And so here we go. I think it is fair to say that I have been failed at every step by the Australian healthcare system both by Federal and State. At the federal level, the role is primarily to provide safe and effective primary care. And so I visited my GP twice, and twice he took no effective action. Suggesting to someone who is psychotic that they are not well and should take medication which is associated with batteries is not clever. Releasing them back into the community is not clever. Who knows what would have happened if I had not gone back to see a different GP and got the referral to see the psychiatrist for an assessment. And this is where the federal government responsibility ends. Please someone correct me if I am wrong on this.

Over to the state government's role. Should I call myself a taxi? Well, the psychiatrist I saw whilst I was psychotic should, in my opinion, be struck off. Allowing me into the general community, seriously? And such a low dose of Seroquel which resulted in my being psychotic for a further four months - after having had the appointment with him!

And then the state hospital system - seeing a psychiatrist for half an hour every two months and being told nothing about what has happened to you, what is happening to you and what may happen to you in the future - if only I was making this up. Moreover no support, advice, anything.

I found some information on the Victorian Department of Health website that notes that some $1.2 billion of taxpayers' money is spent on mental health services across the state each year. At the time of writing this, there was a programme of reform underway consisting of:

- reforming mental health legislation
- strengthening clinical mental health services
- reforming community mental health support services; and
- broadening prevention and promotion activities.

Well, to be honest, there is a lot of work to do. The mental health system is a disaster and everyone who works in it acknowledges this but they feel powerless to do anything. The state and federal government just continue to put their heads in the sand and for this they should be held to account. After all, it could be a member of their family, a close friend, a past acquaintance, an old school friend, a future partner - who know what life holds for any of us. The least we could do is provide support for those when they are at their most vulnerable. And that is not happening. And sadly the state of Victoria is not unique – this is happening worldwide – and it seriously has to stop. Suicide is one of the highest causes of premature death and it is primarily due to the fact that mental health services have, for decades, been under-resourced.

I have basically had to take control, to seek out information on what bipolar disorder is and what bipolar disorder does to those in crisis. I have been lucky enough to connect with a social group, through my own initiative, which has given me deep insight into the condition. It has given me the opportunity to meet with many others living in and around Melbourne who have similar tales to tell, similar experiences and similar questions.

Some have had awful experiences with different GPs and psychiatrists. Some have been on a roller-coaster of medication as a result of which they have lost their authenticity and personality and struggle through each day in a drug-induced fuzziness.

For those asking, is there not a system in place to help people experiencing a mental health crisis? Well, apparently there is. I was informed about this two years after I came out of my psychosis by a friendly social worker attached to my local community health service who I had just commenced regular visits with. The system is: patient is identified and diagnosed either by GP or through ED and then "sectioned" - detained against their free will (this is where I feel a little shaky and think maybe it was better that my GP let me walk out of his practice).

The aim of this detention is to place the individual who is demonstrating psychotic symptoms in a secure (psychiatric) hospital environment where they can be medicated and subsequently monitored and subsequently discharged, once they are considered "stable". When a patient is considered ready for discharge, they are placed into PARC – Prevention and Recovery Care. This is a "step-down" facility to enable the individual to rebuild their skills and confidence and facilitate their re-introduction back into daily life in the broader community.

The mental health system may look from above like a well-designed system. Perusing the State Department of Health's website, you may think would be a first port of call to try and understand how the system is supposed to work but I have given up trying to understand the jumble of links and headlines and announcements. This is how I read it, though I could be wrong. There is a Chief Psychiatrist for the state of Victoria. Whilst I do not here

detail the contents for copyright reasons, you can if you wish check out the webpage:
http://www.health.vic.gov.au/chiefpsychiatrist/index.htm

On this same webpage there is a link to Mental Approved Health Services in Victoria – handy if you feel the need to check yourself in, a link to Outcome Measurement in Mental Health – this is prime comedy for anyone who has had any experience of the mental health services in Victoria and I recommend you explore this page – it is fascinating reading, and a link to a Statement of Rights for those being treated under the Mental Health Act (I guess as I was not being treated under this I had no rights!!!) I, sadly can find no details on how the mental health system is supposed to work but have subsequently found out at my GP practice, that had I gone to a different GP, if he considered I was demonstrating symptoms of psychosis, he would have gone to get a second opinion and then if the diagnosis was validated then I would have been escorted down the road to the main hospital – that is – sectioned!

As I have said previously (and emphasise that this point is not sadly unique to Victoria) the mental health system itself is deeply flawed and everyone knows this. As with all federal and state matters, there is overlap and there are gaps. Everyone has their role but focuses too much on their own rather than that of the individual they are serving. Money is wasted, blame is apportioned and no-one truly takes control to transform the system and so people suffer needlessly. There are too many deaths, whether it be through police failure or through suicide or failure to identify those at risk or through lack of properly funded facilities to support people to recover.

In simple terms we have General Practitioners (the key word here being general) who are federally funded and very much practise to their own abilities and standards. Then we have the community mental health practitioners, state-funded, under-resourced and limited in what they can and do do. And then the hospital system, again under-funded and limited in capacity and capability to deal with mental health and mental illness. Psychologists and Counsellors also play a role and I hear there are some wonderful people out there doing some wonderful work – the challenge is to find them.

If you are happy to pay someone $150 for a 55-minute chat, go ahead. Myself, I have learned that exploring what local library services have to offer provides tons more value. Psychiatrists are supposedly the acknowledged gurus of mental illness, the men with the medicine. The men who can prescribe you everything and anything to take you from heaven to hell and back again as many times as you wish. And they are funded by the state through money collected from those who pay taxes.

Additional services I drew on during my recovery included social workers, though they have a limited understanding of mental illness and mental health and a limited role in supporting individuals on their road to recovery. So it is pretty much up to the psychiatrist, the patient and the pills. Oh me oh my!!

A final cog in the wheel of Australia's mental health framework, the National Mental Health Commission is a Federal Government funded body set up on 1 January 2012 "to report independently to the Prime Minister on what's working and what's not". If you wish to explore more about this body, and it has done some good work in shedding light on what is happening in the mental health sectors across the states and territories, I recommend checking out their website. More details on their role and their work can be found at:

http://www.mentalhealthcommission.gov.au/

Sadly, this body's role is somewhat limited in that all it can do is report. Hopefully with the announcement by the Coalition Government early in 2014 of a review of mental health services across States and Territories, some improvement will finally arrive for those who have been waiting way too long.

Australia also has a set of National Mental Health

Service Standards. First produced in 1998 and revised in 2010, they contain standards on:
- Rights and responsibilities
- Safety
- Consumer and carer participation
- Diversity responsiveness
- Promotion and prevention
- Consumers & Carers
- Governance, leadership and management
- Integration
- Delivery of care

This is classic government - and I write this having examined how government works over some twenty-plus years - if it looks alright from the top it must be alright at the bottom. Well, dear politicians, ministers and Governments of all shades and colours - it doesn't, it's killing people and we would like this to stop.

And whilst researching this chapter, I also found something entitled "Quality in Healthcare", and a body called the "Australian Commission on Safety in improving mental health services". Their website notes, "The Commission has a strong commitment to promote, support and encourage safety and quality in the provision of mental health services. In 2011, the Mental Health Team was established to ensure a greater integrated focus across existing Commission programs."

The Victorian Government is endeavouring to rectify the situation by implementing a series of reforms. The State Government released a document entitled, "Victoria's priorities for mental health reform 2013-15", and again, another worthy document in words and pictures but again no real desire to appropriately fund nor support adequately the scale of reform required to meet the needs of the people. For anyone wishing to read more on what the document contains, please following the link below: http://www.health.vic.gov.au/healthvictoria/feb14/priority.

htm

Well, all I can say to this is they have got a challenge on their hands and it cannot be addressed by State Government alone. Federal Government has a key role to play as well in ensuring GPs are sufficiently competent to be able to identify and treat those experiencing mental illness. Currently this is a major weakness in health systems – worldwide. This is probably why the incidence of suicide is one the major causes of premature death. If only someone in Government would take mental health seriously. It impacts the individual, the family, friends, and local communities. Investment in better mental health services could deliver such major benefits – such as higher rates of health and wellbeing, higher rates of employment, higher rates of productivity through the fostering of a more inclusive and empowered workforce and increased economic growth through engaging more creative minds. There is an argument that those who experience mental illness see the world differently and that once this difference is explored, greatness can and often is achieved; just Google "famous mental illness" and see what comes up!

The question I occasionally ask myself though, is would I have fared any better in the UK. Would my GP have been sufficiently astute to identify the significance of my erratic behaviour? Would they have been able to take appropriate action? Would I have been taken to a mental health facility which was providing "safe and effective" care?

While on the one hand, some argue that the field of mental health and mental illness is still a relatively new and little understood area of healthcare, it is also pretty safe to say that it has been continuously and by successive Governments, under-funded and under-supported.

Mental health and wellbeing is treated too often as a fluffy subject, first in line to be cut and last on the list with regard to ensuring the respecting of an individual's humans rights.

Moreover there is much evidence that our mental health and wellbeing and our physical health are inter-related. The ongoing obesity epidemic is, some argue, a result of our lack of self-respect for our own minds and bodies, a need to seek instantaneous comfort and a lack of understanding of the impact that the contents of what many are eating is not only killing our bodies slowly but also decaying our minds.

To add to the mix the challenges faced by those seeking help in addressing their mental health, they also have to deal with the potential stigma that may or may not arise in their course of seeking treatment. The challenge was reported by the ABC and I have included below as an indication of the scale of the problem.

"Mental health stigma still affecting Australian workers, with research showing 4 in 10 hide depression from employers.

Four out of 10 Australians who take sick leave for depression keep it hidden from their employer, with almost half fearing their job would be compromised if they revealed their illness..."

"Beyond Blue chief executive Kate Carnell says the statistics are "very worrying", but it would be illegal for an employer to sack somebody on the basis of a mental health issue. Ms Carnell says Australian employers have a legal responsibility to provide a "psychologically safe workplace."

"Employers have an obligation under occupational health and safety legislation to have a mental health friendly workplace," she said.

"It's important for workplaces to have mental-health policy in place and also to have leadership - to make it clear to employees that they will treat mental health the same way they treat physical health issues."

Ms Carnell agrees that stigma in the workplace is still a particular issue.

"What's important is that workplaces make it clear

that we encourage employees to put their hands up early, and if they start to struggle to let their supervisors know and for business to have in place a method to support those people," she said.

"Stigma is still a real issue - we are getting better as a community but we are not there yet. "[We] need to focus on reducing that stigma, but particularly in the workplace."

Ms Carnell says reducing mental illness issues in the workplace will not only benefit workers, but is essential to boosting productivity in Australia.

"If you can support [workers] early then there is a good chance they won't end up having to have time of, which is of course a cost to the workplace and the employee as well," she said.

"The cost to Australian workplaces now exceeds $12 billion. Last year, stress-related work compensation issues topped $10 billion, so mental-health issues are costing Australian businesses significant dollars.

"We need to make it clear to employers that having a mental-health safe workplace is not only the law, but it will also help increase productivity, achieve their bottom line, reduce staff turnover and absenteeism, so everybody is a winner. "

Source:
http://www.abc.net.au/news/2013-11-12/australians-worried-depression-will-cost-their-job-study/5085820

I have read too many books which recount tales where patients have suffered at the hands of clinicians. As I note in the title of this chapter - You have to take control even when you are not in control. One of the most inspiring books I have read on this journey has been "You - the Smart Patient: An insider's handbook on getting the best treatment" by Michael F Roizen M.D. and Mehmet C Oz M.D. The following is a direct quote:

"The Advisory Commission on Consumer Protection

and Quality in the Health Care Industry created a 'Consumer Bill of Rights and Responsibilities'. The Joint Commission...ensures that health care organisations respect your rights when providing care, treatment and services to you or your family. Here are just a few of the basic entitlements you enjoy as a patient in our fair land [please note this is the U.S. - but I feel it could apply to any other countries, please also note some of the content also contains humour in places]:

- as a patient, you have the right to considerate, respectful care. You aren't obligated to be considerate and respectful to those who are caring for you, but it would be nice;
- you have the right to obtain current, understandable, relevant information about your diagnosis, treatment and prognosis from health care providers. Rather than waiting for it to be handed to you, though we'd suggest exercising your right to seek it out on your own. if you add objective and complete to the adjectives above;
- if you speak another language, have a disability, or don't understand something you have the right to have it explained to you so you do understand it. This doesn't mean that doctors have to give you the answer that'll make you happy, however;
- you have the right to immediate emergency screening and stabilisation when you're in severe pain or have been injured. Of course, immediate could mean sixteen hours if the ER is really backed up the night;
- except in emergencies where you must be treated right away, you have the right to discuss your treatment options, the benefits and risks involved, the length of recuperation and medical alternatives before making a decision about your care. You even have the right to discuss this with so many doctors, consultants and alternative medical

practitioners that you might never get round to making any decisions;
- you have the right to know the identity of the people involved in caring for you as well as their experience, such as if they're new residents or students. You can attempt to flirt with them as well, but it may not get you better treatment;
- you have the right to know the estimated costs of all treatments. You also have the right to be given ice water and a cold compress after fainting upon learning the estimated costs;
- you have the right to make decisions about the care you'll receive and to refuse certain treatments to the extent permitted by law. In the best situation, you won't have angry relatives trying to have you declared insane;
- you have the right to expect that your medical information will be kept confidential, except in cases where reporting is require by law. For an example of the latter, if you have Ebola virus, we have to report it. But you won't have long to be upset anyway;
- you have the right to an advance directive such as a living will, durable power of attorney for health care or health care proxy;
- you have the right to review your medical records and have the information in them explained to you. You may also express consternation if your medicals are presented to you in seven large supermarket paper bags, and you're given a pitchfork to sort through them;
- in a hospital setting, you have the right to receive medical care within a reasonable time. Reasonable is a much longer span of time than immediate, and immediate is subject to the interpretation explained in the previous right;
- you have the right to refuse to agree or refuse to

participate in research studies and to have them fully explained to you before you jump in. This doesn't guarantee that a treatment will be named after you, however.

A shocking piece of research conducted by the Personal Social Services Research Unit (PSSRU) at the universities of Kent and London School of Economics, revealed quite staggering cuts in the provision of social care for people with mental health problems in England. The study, which was commissioned by the Care and Support Alliance, a consortium of more than 70 charities and organisations representing older and disabled people, found that after adjusting for socio-demographic changes, the number of people with mental health problems receiving social care had dropped by 48% since 2005. It also found that one in three local authorities had reduced mental health services by at least 50%. The cuts were, the study concluded, "almost certainly without precedent in the history of adult social care". There have also been substantial cuts in social care provision for older people (39%, after standardisation) and people with physical disabilities (33%, ditto) but in a worryingly familiar pattern, mental health services have once again been targeted disproportionately. The PSSRU study estimates that the cuts are equivalent to 63,000 fewer people with mental health problems receiving social care since 2005."

More on this research can be explored by checking out the following link:
http://www.theguardian.com/society/2014/apr/01/mental-health-cuts-cost-more-than-save

There is so much written about the impact of poor mental health, the toll is places on individuals, families, communities, business, workplaces and local economies. The UK Government introduced a concept of parity of esteem, whereby physical and mental health are to be provided the same weight of importance in all areas of policy-making and service delivery. Unyet, whilst noble in words, there is yet to be any solid commitment from the UK government as to how this is to be achieved. There is a huge disparity between the amount of taxpayer money allocated to treating physical conditions and that allocated to mental health. I guess the ideal scenario would be where mental health was a priority from earliest schooling, through all stages of childhood development and on through all subsequent life stages. One fascinating comment I overheard on a bus once regarded parenthood, people are required to be qualified to drive a car, practise a profession or fly a plane, but there is no training or qualification to support those entering parenthood/ guardianship, possibly the most important role anyone one could have?

I looked into what had been written about mental health and include below a couple of articles online highlighting the scale of the issue:

"Mental health services need targeted investment, not even more cuts
By 2030, there will be an estimated two million more adults with a mental health problem. So, what should the new NHS England chief executive Simon Stevens's priorities be when it comes to improving mental health in the NHS?"
Source:
http://www.theguardian.com/society/2014/mar/26/mental-health-investment-not-cuts-nhs-simon-stevens

"Mental health: the last workplace taboo
A culture of silence on mental health in the workplace causes suffering and discrimination. Some businesses aim to tackle it."
Mental health is one of the biggest threats to the wellbeing of business and society.Employees across the UK are working harder and are under more pressure than ever before.

Yet there remains a culture of silence around mental health at work and businesses are reluctant to report publicly on the proactive steps that are being taken to foster mental wellbeing. Employers and employees are unwilling to talk about stress, anxiety and depression openly, fearful of any association with weakness and failure."

Source:
http://www.theguardian.com/sustainable-business/mental-health-taboo-workplace-employers

Chapter 5
We are all bipolar - is that not a good thing?

Controversial? Well sometimes you have to be to get someone's attention. And that has been the problem for far too long. Do we truly pay attention to what we are doing? Do we consciously track our thoughts? Our decisions? Our actions? Are we constantly adding value in all that we do each and every day? Or do we go off track? Do we make decisions that do not add value to our lives? There is an approach in the field of evaluation called The Logic Model - the model consists of inputs, processes, outputs and outcomes, framed within what is called an environment. In terms of our life journey, the following could be used to apply the logic model to our lives:

- inputs: diet, exercise, learning, reading, money, love, oxygen
- processes: eating at regular meal times (5 a day), exercise (20 minutes, 5 times a week at least), reading a book a month which enhances our understanding of ourselves and the world around us, participating in healthy and rewarding relationships;
- outputs: feeling a sense of achievement on an ongoing basis, thinking in a measured manner using all available information to hand at the time whilst also connecting with gut instinct in making decisions, adding value to our self-worth and the self-worth of those around us;
- outcomes: enabling our lives to fulfil our potential, ensuring we feel enriched in every sense and minimising the occurrence of any risks that life may present whilst at the same time empowering us to have strength of mind and heart to work through anything and everything with a calm and compassionate self-awareness;

- environment: the area in which live, the places we visit, the laws with which we are required and expect to comply, the weather, the quality of the air and light.

So why do I say we are all bipolar? Well, let's discuss. There is much evidence that whilst stress is healthy for us in measured quantities (whatever that means), too much stress can be harmful. But how much is too much? And how can we know whether, in the moment, we are stressed or not? And how can we rewire our minds to allow ourselves to better deal with stress and the impact that it can have on our lives?

The reason I suggest we are all bipolar is that there is a theory, and it is still early days in terms of research but those looking into the world of bipolar have suggested there could be up to six different categories of the disorder and maybe more. After all, how many times have you got up in the morning feeling exhausted, had to charge yourself up with coffee and then dragged yourself into work to maintain a level of activity only to experience another energy slump around mid-morning. Is that your body or your mind telling you something? Is your body short of what it needs to function effectively or is it stressed or telling you, "enough already - I need a break from all this!"

If we tracked our energy throughout the day, throughout the week, throughout the month, throughout the year - would we notice a pattern? If we mapped out in a diary: key events, key dates or levels of stress we were feeling against our energy and then made tweaks to our lifestyles such as taking a little bit of time out, focusing a little more on "me time", on rewarding relationships friendships, on diet and exercise - would we notice any changes, any connections between how we were investing in ourselves and how we were feeling about ourselves?

Bipolar disorder is considered an extreme mental disorder. However it could be considered that in many ways, the way we live could indicate many of us are living a "bipolar life". After all, have we not at times lived in the fast lane and then crashed, have we not pushed the boundaries perhaps a little further than we should - and then suffered the consequences? Was this to be expected or was this a total shock?

One of the most intriguing things that happened whilst I was psychotic was that I decided to become a life coach. I attended the intake weekend of a Diploma in Life Coaching whilst psychotic - I had no idea I was psychotic and neither did those around me. I guess they just thought I had quite an outgoing personality and was quite vivacious. But if this happened with me, how many people are experiencing the very same experiences at this very moment in time? How many times have you driven into work and had no recollection of how you got there? How many times have you slipped into auto-pilot - or rather, your brain has slipped into auto-pilot whilst another part of your brain is focusing on something completely different, or maybe having a little daydream or fantasy - whatever - how often have you found this occurring in your daily life? Should it be cause for concern? Well if you are a risk to yourself or someone else - I guess it should be. After all, how many road accidents have been caused by drivers not being aware of what is happening around them? And what impact does "multiple-thinking" have on our minds (doing one thing whilst thinking about something completely different)? To what extent are we truly present and aware of what is happening around us? And what is the point of not being present? After all is that not what life is all about, living for the moment and enjoying all that life has to offer? Whilst at times it may not seem like you are the captain of your ship, if you look back across your journey to this point, you may find that the majority of factors that contributed to your current state of being are a result of each and every decision you had previously made.

I am trying to steer away from too much woo woo here but forgive me if I stray a little into it.

One of the most wonderful books I read during my recovery was a book entitled *Acceptance: An Insider's guide of Bipolar Disorder* by Johnathan C Barker. In this book the author provides great insight into the condition and how he dealt with the various challenges presented to him in getting back on his feet. One of the biggest was developing the ability to accept what is. This has been one of the most challenging aspects of recovering from the psychotic episode I experienced. Being someone who has been fairly driven in the past, and having the knowledge of what I can achieve, the memories of what I have achieved and the constant head pains and exhaustion that result in my having to almost, on a daily basis, take midday naps often lasting 2-3 hours and having to endure head pains that move around inside my skull, change in intensity and which bear no relationship to what I am doing, have been doing or have been thinking of doing - acceptance is huge.

Whilst typing this chapter, I hopped over to Google and typed into the search box - "we are all bipolar" to see what results might appear. One interesting "conversational thread" I include below:

"Are We All A Bit Bipolar?

A - I have one strange question and that is - are we all a bit bipolar? I'm asking this for it happens sometimes that I kind of a feel some weird symptoms that run from high enthusiasm to such hopelessness I couldn't describe it's like I'm little crazy and little depressed depends on I don't know what. So what do you think, are we all a bit bipolar?

B - Yes, yes, I know how you must be feeling. I'm positive on this and am totally convinced that we all are a bit bipolar, it's just thing of a control I also in myself occasionally could recognize those symptoms, for there are days in which I feel so euphoric and overly good, I don't even need sleep and am so active and enthusiastic and happy but after a few days depression grabs me, there's no hope, and everything seems so without any sense. But you know what? I don't know if those symptoms have something to do with bipolarism but I am sure these periods are related. So I've came to a conclusion that we all are a bit bipolar, at least I am bipolar when it comes about my period and then again I'm back to normal track. Any way I think some kind of bipolarism is there in all of us and it's just that in someone's sometime it takes more severe forms that needs to be treated and I think I'm of the ones who can control itself well, kind of a like I know how to deal with these occasional "symptoms".

C - no one is totally completely normal!

Where do you draw the line between being nervous in around people and being sociopathic?

Who can draw the line when someone stops having little quirks and having an obsessive compulsive disorder?

Where is that tiny threshold between paranoid and insane? who is allowed to say what the limit is?

We are all mentally ill in one way or another, even if it's to a tiny degree, the people who get professional help with their problems are the ones who have it so bad it interferes in their day to day life. but just because it doesn't interfere with your day to day activities doesn't mean you can't get angry, or depressed, or freaked out etc.

No one is completely normal, human beings wouldn't be human otherwise, we all have quirks and compulsions in our behaviour.

D - I would totally agree!

I think mental illnesses have become very "popular" recently and some things like extreme emotions get given a label, like depression or bi-polar disorder.

Obviously being bi-polar is horrible as the people who suffer from it feel very extreme high and low emotions but i think it is natural for everyone to have extreme emotions at one point or another.

E - No I definitely disagree. Bipolar is a horrible life-changing mental disorder that is petrifying. The 'similarities' between non-bipolar people and bipolar people are probably just because moods are a part of our brain makeup, we need them and they are completely normal, even if they seem extreme or irrational. Bipolar moods are not like 'normal' moods. They're terrifying and either extreme can lead to death, humiliation or alienation from friends and family."

Another article I found I cite below:
"Imagine you're at University and you have your first manic episode. You think you are just partying too hard but things get out of control - you can't sleep and your thoughts are racing. You are admitted to hospital and told you have Bipolar Disorder.

The message you get is that Bipolar Disorder (BD) is a mental illness with unpredictable periods of extreme high and low mood. You'll never fully recover but daily medication can reduce the frequency of episodes. Unfortunately the medication has nasty side effects and you're likely to have more episodes over time. Only half of people with BD work consistently, it's associated with the highest rates of divorce and suicide of all psychiatric diagnoses, and to manage it you need to avoid stress, late nights, drugs and alcohol.

How do you feel? Many people are frightened, defeated and hopeless. They change their lives as advised and take the tablets, maybe dropping out of University to avoid stress. This means giving up life aspirations triggering feelings of failure and low mood - a self-fulfilling prophecy.

What if this message is wrong? Is there a message that acknowledges the difficulties while highlighting positive aspects? It could emphasise positive lifestyle changes and relapse prevention while still pursuing dreams. It might reveal a wider range of outcomes - not just inevitable

decline. If you got this message instead would it change things? Might you stay at University?"
Source:
http://www.lancaster.ac.uk/news/blogs/fiona-lobban/bipolar-disorder—we-need-a-more-balanced-perspective/

Is it no wonder that mental health has such stigma attached to it and that so many people either:
- hide symptoms;
- hide thoughts;
- hide themselves;
- fear judgement;
- fear stigma;
- fear themselves and what is happening to them through no fault of their own but as a result of how their brain chemistry is quirkily responding resulting in thoughts, decisions and behaviour of which they can make no rational sense?

And an article from CNN I found online which I feel highlights many of the issues I have experienced personally and is why, as I move forward in my life, highlighting the importance of good mental health and removing the stigma attached to mental illness will become my core in all I do. Herewith said article:

"I lost my husband to Bipolar Disorder.
Before he got sick, my husband, Mike", was one of the warmest, funniest guys around. He was a great talker who could engage with anyone about anything - Czech history one minute, 1950s monster movies the next.
The two of us had countless in-jokes, and our conversations always seemed to devolve into laughter.
But in April 1996, 12 years after we had first started dating, Mike said something that wasn't funny

at all.

"See that guy over there?" he whispered to me in a voice so low I had to lean closer to hear. "He thinks I'm CIA." Mike and I had arrived a few hours earlier for our vacation in Saigon, exhausted and bleary-eyed after 22 hours of flying from our home in New York City. We had eaten dinner and were sipping beers in the café at our hotel. I glanced in the direction Mike was staring. All I saw was a 20-something Vietnamese man reading a magazine.

There was no way that this man, I thought, Mike - a curly-haired, jeans and T-shirt -clad freelance copy editor - was in the CIA. Then I looked into Mike's eyes. His pupils were completely dilated. I felt unsteady. Mike just peered at me, his eyes wide with fear.

I could see that something was wrong with him, but I didn't know what. I was naïve; mental illness didn't even cross my mind. I simply thought that if we could cut our vacation short and get him back to familiar surroundings in New York, everything would be fine.

But Mike calmed down, insisting that he was OK and that he wanted to stay in Vietnam. I complied, as I often did.

In those days, I was painfully passive, certain that it was best for both of us that Mike made the decisions. And for much of the rest of the trip, I was grateful that we hadn't taken drastic action.

Mike was back to his delightful and charming self. We had pho for lunch one day (a noodle soup pronounced "fuh") and made up puns about it. "I'd fuh-gotten how tasty this is," Mike said to me, and I laughed.

However, I purposely ignored some of his more curious behaviors: checking the hotel locks and windows multiple times; shushing me, even when we were alone in our room. He had never acted like this before, what I didn't realize was that a new paranoia had taken up residence in Mike's mind - and it was never going away.

Mike and I met in 1983, when we were college students in New Orleans.

Our relationship turned romantic quickly.

We'd sit in the sun in his quad or mine or read books side by side on his futon, snuggled under his childhood tiger-print blanket.

After graduation, we travelled for a year, strapping on backpacks and bumming around various parts of the world.

Then, in 1987, we moved to Manhattan, where we both got jobs and shared an apartment. We didn't really have separate lives: we'd often meet for lunch just to catch up on the few hours we'd spent apart. Neither of us went out without the other. If Mike was meeting up with his friends, I'd tag along. If I had a girls' night planned, Mike would come, too. I was terribly insecure.

I didn't feel smart or clever, and I knew that Mike was smart and clever. So I deferred to him whenever I could. Once I wanted to try a yoga class. So I spent hours convincing Mike to come along. It didn't occur to me that I could try a class on my own. We even shared an e-mail account. It was only years later, as Mike grew ill, that I realized that my dependency was unhealthy.

When we returned home to New York after our trip to Saigon, Mike seemed normal.

But a few months later, when Mike was 33, his strange behavior returned.

At first the changes were subtle.

We had a crate where we kept important papers - tax forms, passports - and he became obsessed with rummaging through it.

His voice changed, too, in a way that was imperceptible to anyone but me. His tone was deadened. When he joked, he lacked his previous enthusiasm.

I only began to worry in earnest on the night he stayed out until dawn, without warning. When he finally came back, he kissed me on the forehead like he'd just finished a day at the office.

Furious, I told him how distraught I'd been. In response, all he said was, "It's OK. I was out for a stroll." Then he shot me an eerie, fake smile.

None of this was like Mike.

I suddenly wondered what else he might do: would he make an offensive comment to a stranger and trigger a fight? Would he wander into traffic? Increasingly concerned, I called his parents, who lived in New Jersey and didn't know anything had been the matter with their son.

An hour later, they pulled up in front of our building, and we drove straight to the family's primary-care doctor.

He suggested a battery of tests and a hospital stay to rule out physiological explanations for Mike's behavior.

But he clearly suspected mental illness and recommended that Mike go to a psychiatric ward. Shocking though it may seem, that's when it first occurred to me that Mike's mind was the problem. I was both relieved (hey, at least it probably wasn't a brain tumor!) and terrified. Mike was diagnosed with severe depression and was put on an antidepressant"

But he didn't last long in the psych ward. He checked himself out two days after his arrival, insisting he wasn't sick. And after about a month at home, thanks to medication and weekly therapy, Mike again seemed like himself.

I was so optimistic about his recovery, in fact, that about a year later, when he spontaneously asked me to marry him, I said yes. The next day, December 12, 1997, we took our vows at City Hall.

Five months later, I became pregnant.

I was ecstatic at the prospect of starting a family - convinced that we would be fantastic parents and that Mike's illness was behind us for good.

But my sense of certainty was crushed just a few minutes after our daughter, Lizzie, was born, on February 9, 1999. As I lay in the hospital bed. Mike leaned over and said, "I heard the baby talk to me. "

I couldn't believe it: he had gone off his medication without my realizing it.

I begged him to go back on the drugs, and he listened. But he seemed less stable than before, as though he might lose control at any moment.

As in Saigon, he constantly checked our locks and shushed me. He struggled to bond with Lizzie. He held her in a rocking chair and read her books but often had a totally blank expression on his face.

I never felt comfortable leaving Lizzie alone with Mike. His mind always seemed elsewhere. When Lizzie was about 14 months old, Mike went off his medication yet again and was hospitalized.

This time he received a new diagnosis, the one he still has today: severe bipolar disorder, which is a mental illness characterized by long periods of depression followed by shorter bouts of mania.

The diagnosis scared me. Although about 5.7 million Americans have bipolar disorder, I'd never known someone with it.

Perhaps for that reason, I saw the disease as shameful. I couldn't bear to tell my mom and dad, or my friends, that Mike was no longer just "depressed."

Meanwhile, Mike wasn't getting better.

Instead of nine good months at a time, he'd have five, then two - largely because he kept refusing to take his Zyprexa pills, swearing that he wasn't ill.

Panicked, I visited countless doctors, read countless books, and visited support groups in an effort to find him (and myself) real help.

Mike didn't want to hear about any of it. He stopped working and spent hours lying on the floor, listening to "Ziggy Stardust" over and over.

Then one weekend, in the spring of 2002, I reached a tipping point.

Mike was driving the two of us to a nearby grocery store" He seemed a bit withdrawn but still communicative. So I was unprepared when, suddenly, he blew through a stop sign.

I shouted for him to brake, but he didn't seem to hear. "STOP!" I screamed again. Petrified, after he ran another" When he finally did stop, I got out of the car and walked home, shaken. I didn't know what to do. The answer became clear the next day, when our family went to the park. Three-year-old Lizzie held out her hands to Mike, shouting, "Daddy, up!" He just walked right by her, and I saw her face fall.

That night, as I tucked her into bed, she said, "I don't like Daddy really much." Her words got to me. What kind of example was I setting by not putting my daughter first? I made a silent vow to take control of my life.

One day later, I stood before a New York City Supreme Court judge and requested to have Mike committed. I told him, voice quavering, that Mike was a danger to himself and others, citing the stop-sign incident and his inconsistency with his medication as evidence. The order was granted.

Police officers came to our apartment and took Mike to the hospital, he resisted at first, but eventually the officers convinced him to comply. I told Mike that if he stayed there and got help - and kept going to his psychiatrist after he was released - I'd be there for him. If not, I'd leave. I knew what would happen, and it did: he checked himself out of the hospital after 48 hours (which was legal under the terms of the commitment order). And true to my word, I took Lizzie and left.

Six months later, I filed for legal separation, and two years after that we divorced.

It wasn't easy: I held on to a lot of guilt for ending the marriage.

I felt that I shouldn't have abandoned someone who was ill, someone whom I had loved for so long. I felt it was my duty to make Mike better.

However, I also was relieved - for me and for Lizzie.

To her, Mike had been so emotionally absent that his physical disappearance seemed like the next logical step.

As for me, I felt like a great weight had been lifted, and I could finally enjoy life again. I remember walking down the street feeling like I could float away.

After the marriage ended, I needed to talk about Mike's mental illness.

It was as if I'd explode if I didn't. I found I was far from alone.

One friend told me about her debilitating post-partum depression. An acquaintance, who was married with two kids, told me she had bipolar disorder.

But she saw a therapist regularly and understood that she needed medication. Her case made me fully understand the severity of Mike's condition and of his denial.

Seventeen years into his illness, Mike still cycles on and off his medications.

When he's off, he tends to fixate on bizarre ideas. (He's prone to announcing via e-mail that he's an heir to an oil fortune or a Mayflower descendant.)

Mike's mother, with whom I remain close, is his legal guardian and helps him function. He still cannot work.

I've moved on. I married a wonderful man, Jeff, who has been a full parent to Lizzie.

Our relationship is truly equal: We make all our decisions together.

Lizzie and I see Mike only about once a year, due to his erratic behavior. And in between visits we don't keep in touch. I hear about Mike periodically through his mother. Lizzie knows that he has bipolar disorder and that there's a genetic component to the illness.

"Will I get it?" she asked me a few years ago, when she was 11. I told her probably not, but that, regardless, it's usually treatable. We talk openly; I never want her to feel mental illness is something that should be hidden, as I once did.

But I also don't want her to believe that an increased chance of mental illness is the only thing she inherited from Mike.

So I tell her about his keen intelligence, our exciting travels and the relationship we once shared. And when she laughs and jokes, sometimes I catch a glimpse of that man, my first love. It's a bittersweet moment, but one I wouldn't trade for the world.

Source:
http://edition.cnn.com/2013/07/24/health/change-mind-real-simple

Gus O'Donnell, former head of the civil service in the UK wrote in The Guardian in April 2014 a useful addition to the debate on mental health and wellbeing:

"Focus on wellbeing - an alternative cure for the NHS's ills

Better prevention, as well as better treatment, can be achieved by government departments joining forces

The Department of Health (DH) faces an enormous challenge: how to meet ever-increasing demand from an ageing society while public spending increases no faster than inflation. And maybe less fast: last month's budget implies further public expenditure cuts, to meet the government's deficit targets.

The "solution" most often proposed is further below-inflation pay rises for NHS staff, more reconfiguration of hospitals and new ways of enhancing productivity. There is no alternative? Well, actually this time there is: but it involves a radical change of focus, a Whitehall shake up, and some tough spending choices.

The drive to improve productivity has led to ever-more emphasis on "output" measures for the NHS: numbers of operations performed, or patients tested. But the inadequacies of this approach have heightened interest in a wider concept: life satisfaction, or "wellbeing". In a recent report "Wellbeing and Policy", commissioned by the Legatum Institute, my fellow economists and I recommend making wellbeing the government's overriding objective when designing policy.

This would require a huge change of priorities for the DH: first, shifting attention from physical to mental health, making a reality of the department's theoretical commitment to equal status for both.

Mental illness accounts for an enormous amount of suffering, or loss of wellbeing. And it is estimated that three-quarters of it goes untreated. To tackle this requires not just money, but also a joined-up approach with the Department for Education. There should be a minister for mental health with a seat in both departments, complementing better treatment with better prevention, through programmes to promote emotional and social development in schools. In fact, there would need to be a general emphasis on prevention of illness. As many as four-fifths of deaths from major diseases are mainly the result of lifestyle factors, such as smoking, drinking and obesity." Far more of the budget needs to be directed at reducing those risks, and not just through increased financial investment: this is an area desperately in need of a combination of private-sector innovation and smart regulation.

Take road safety. Since the 1930s, the number of cars on our roads - and the number of miles we drive - has risen enormously. Yet far fewer people are killed on the roads.

Innovations in car design, road design and driving regulations, backed up by social pressures, have helped to transform road safety. Today, three times as many people die from suicide as in motor vehicle accidents. Now we need to focus on preventing these tragedies with the same combination of skills.

Such changes won't be easy, because even if they yield savings in the long term, they will require money to be cut from other parts of the health budget in the short term. But the third essential change will be, institutionally, even harder.

Health services and social care need to be brought much closer together. That is more or less accepted. More controversially, the DH should be given part of the budget for disability benefits, so it focuses on getting people back to work. This would help the reallocation of resources to both physical and psychological therapies. Higher employment rates among disabled people may look like an old-style, output-driven measure of success. It isn't. For not only would their work contribute to higher GDP, it would have a powerful effect on their wellbeing. One of the clearest insights from wellbeing research is that unemployment has a huge psychological cost. (In fact, making adjustments for various disabilities is a lot cheaper than most employers realise and such workers tend to be very loyal.)

Other Whitehall departments should also review their priorities. But health shows the opportunities, and the challenges, of defining, measuring and pursuing the wellbeing of the nation as a whole. It's a great place to start on this essential journey of policy reform."

Source:
http://www.theguardian.com/society/2014/apr/01/wellbeing-alternative-cure-nhs-health

Chapter 6

What next - even if your world collapses, another door opens

One of the fascinating things about this whole adventure is the fact that I have got to where I am, in my view, despite of not because of the systems put in place to support those in crisis; I admit I have been, in many ways, in a living hell. Daily taking medication which you are told nothing about and the side effects of which lead to you feeling exhausted and cause ongoing pain within your skull is a living nightmare. No-one gives you any warning. It's like jumping off a cliff without a parachute and hoping for the best.

My recovery has been one of trial and error. After six months or thereabouts of being, let's be honest about it, completely bonkers - I came out of the psychosis to find myself not living in my apartment, with a steady but enjoyable and rewarding job, a fun social life and an amenable existence. All my friends disappeared. Most of my belongings are in storage.

And I am now in shared accommodation in a room surrounded by what could not be crammed into the storage unit.

Ironically, during my psychotic episode, I decided to become a life coach. From money my wonderful mum had sent me over from the UK, I was able to use some to pay some of the outstanding rent and use the rest to pay for the deposit for the course and away I went on the intake weekend. Three days of training of which I can remember very little. Hardly anything. Apart from some weird conversations during morning or afternoon breaks about my having a balloon which was expanding and floating up into the air like my business. Oh yes, and I had planned out a training event in which each attendee would choose from a selection of fruit and vegetables and that the event would take the form of a play. How could they not have known I was completely off my rocker!

I should have taken time out from this path on which I had decided to embark but I persisted, not really understanding what I had signed up for nor having much idea of how long it would take me to recover from the psychosis.

And so I embarked on the journey to becoming a life coach. This involved a number of elements including completing papers (some 21 in total), and fulfilling a number of other requirements, including completing a series of triads. This involved being a member of three teams, one where you were a coach, one where you were a "client", and one where you were a listener. It was quite enjoyable, if a little nerve-wracking.

The results I achieved from the coaching sessions were, for me, fascinating. I was quite intrigued each week to hear the tone and energy in the voice of my "client" and the noticeable changes she was making in her own journey as a result of our coaching sessions, were for me, incredibly rewarding. We had met during our intake weekend and it was only a couple of years later that I revealed to her what I had been and was going through. She had no idea. I also met the trainer who lead the coaching intake weekend several months ago, he also had no idea. Fascinating stuff - you meet someone who is psychotic - they have no idea, you have no idea - life goes on.

I was able to complete the triads pretty smoothly and listened and took notes on the various webinars that formed part of the Diploma course. As 2011 moved into 2012, I was making good progress but then went on lithium and anti-depressants and plunged into a three-month depression. This was one of the worst depressions I have ever experienced. No warning. Go see a psychiatrist. Yes, I think we should put you on some additional medication and write off a further three months of your life. Oh cheers, thanks a lot!

Many a day went by when the head pains were too

great to be bearable. So as a mild anaesthetic, I reached for the vodka bottle. No mixer - straight down. A bottle a day. And slept. It was the only way I could get through the pain. And I don't even like vodka. Well I guess you do what you have to do to get you through.

The rest of 2012 and 2013 are a bit of a blur. Thankfully where I was living was close to somewhere that offered me a wonderful escape and helped me significantly in grappling with my head pains and exhaustion, my depression and the journey I had to embark on in getting myself out of it. Because not only have I been diagnosed with the second most serious mental disorder, I had also been diagnosed HIV+ some ten years previously. This centre played a massive role. I cannot highlight how poor the services are for those grappling with their mental health. There is nothing in my humble opinion to support those grappling with the mental health. NOTHING!

On top of trying to get better whilst dealing with a psychiatrist who was of little help and a GP who truly had little understanding of mental health, I had an elderly mother living in the UK who I had not seen for four years. She had had to endure, at the stage of her life when all stress should be minimised, listening to her only son - who she knew was severely unwell - whilst feeling totally powerless and dealing with her own declining health. She is a warrior and sits quietly whilst I type away; she is in her eighty-eighth year.

Before I left the UK, I remortgaged my flat in London to raise some capital and rented it out to cover the mortgage. This worked for a while but in between a period when I was in and out of depressions, I tried to sell it without truly understanding the extent to which the UK property market had collapsed. And so the debts mounted up. I recall trying to explain to the mortgage company in the UK what I was trying to achieve, whilst they would not accept communication via e-mail whilst they were also keen to repossess the property and get someone in who would boost their profits a bit more than I was doing.

Sadly, I lost the prolonged battle and the property was repossessed in early 2013 with the proceeds being locked away in something called The Courts Funds Office.

Even during my psychosis, I recall phoning Mum each week. Towards the end of 2013, I began to call her more frequently; as her asthma seemed to be getting the better of her, I was becoming increasingly concerned. And then there was the inevitable. I had tried calling several times over the period of a couple of days, when I decided enough was enough and I called the police. Unfortunately I could not work out how to call the local force, so I ended up calling the Metropolitan Police in London and they did a wonderful job. Mum had taken a fall and had been lying, alone, for two days unable to move or call for help.

I have no idea how I kept my calm that night but somehow I managed to track, through regular hourly calls, her progress through Accident and Emergency, Clinical Assessment and subsequently to the ward on which she had been allocated. Further calls had revealed that if I was able to release the money from The Courts Fund Office this would provide sufficient funds to enable me to fly to the UK. And so within the week, I flew halfway across the globe, landing at London Heathrow around lunchtime and after over 20 hours on a plane, travelled three hours north from Kings Cross, arriving at my mum's bedside at some time just after ten in the evening.

She was in hospital for a month. I was in shock. She was so frail and almost at death's door. I had no idea whether she would make it through and I think many of the nursing staff felt the same. As for the doctors, well, they really were unreal - even though I was next of kin, it was as if I did not exist. Subsequent visits ensued. Poor mother, she was in a strange ward with a constantly evolving group of individuals she did not know, being fed food that was beyond awful - the worst was when one of the orderly's plonked a Cornish pasty on her tray - 90% pastry and no gravy. Unreal. With all due respect though, there were some true angels working on the ward and I give due credit to those who know they are doing wonderful things on Ward 6A. It is sad that the ward manager hides away in their office with little desire or willingness to fulfil their role or responsibilities. The hospital itself: a shocker.

I had known for a while about the hospital and the extent to which it was failing to provide safe and effective care. However, as my mum was in their care, I decided to update myself and found the latest Care Quality Commission report on the place. And this is what I read:

"We found staff could not always respond to the need of patients. We found not all care needs were assessed, planned for or delivered in a timely manner. We found that some care records were not updated appropriately such as care plans, risk assessments and hourly observation chats. This means patients were at risk of not receiving consistent or appropriate care.

We found a confusing picture when we looked at how patients, their families and representatives were involved in the decision whether to resuscitate a patient or not. When we looked in the document used for "do not attempt cardio pulmonary resuscitation" we found some poor recording practice, not all records were clear who had been involved in the decision and why, and there were some medical records without details of discussions held.

Staff reported they could not give the care they would wish to do and also keep up with the necessary paperwork. This was causing increased levels of stress, particularly when registered nurses had to undertake additional duties and procedures to cover for newly registered nurses and agency staff.

We found communication at time ineffective between different staff groups including medical and nursing as well as between clinical staff and senior managers at Trust Board level. We found leadership was variable across wards and between ward/

departmental level and senior management. We found some very positive practice taking place, but this was not necessarily shared across the hospital. Staff were not confident in the reporting system, and told us that feedback was inconsistent between managers. One doctor said, "I don't think anything is being fed up to the Board, we occasionally get an e-mail from the medical directorate about an incident telling us not to do something."

The trust has introduced some quality monitoring systems and these were indicating that improvements across care and practice were improving. However, we found some poor performance and high levels of risk had been identified over several months and action taken was ineffective. It was not clear for some performance information that any action had been taken to address issues or drive improvement or that timescales were appropriate. The Trust Board had recently agreed a revised board assurance framework which contained robust reporting and management systems. However, this was not yet fully introduced and embedded in the trust. New strategies had been introduced to improve communication and consultation, including "Listening Events", whereby senior manager including the Chief Executive were meeting with staff groups....

.. In the past three years, the Care Quality Commission has continued to raise its concerns about the quality of care provided by this trust. Improvements have not been sustained. We are aware that the trust has recently been placed in special measures by the NHS Trust Development Authority due to poor quality of care that has been identified.

The trust has already developed an action plan in response to the XXXX's rapid responsive review and this will be monitored by NHS England. The NHS TDA will have the responsibility to support the trust to improve and to take the necessary action to ensure that the issues raised in the XXXX Review are addressed.

In response to the findings in this report, we will also require the trust to show us how it will become safe, effective, caring, responsive and well lead. We will continue to closely monitor the trust, inspecting as required and working with NHS England to review progress.

We have judged that this has a major impact on people who use the service. This is being followed up and we will report on any action when it is complete."

Some might say bury the bad news at the back of a report. And so as I got to the back of the report, I found the following:

"In the past three years, the Care Quality Commission has continued to raise its concerns about the quality of care provided by this trust. Improvements have not been sustained. We are aware that the trust has recently been placed in special measures by the NHS Trust Development Authority due to the poor quality of care that has been identified....

....We looked at this outcome to understand how the Trust Board (the Board) and management team monitored the care and welfare of people who use services at the hospital and how effective their governance systems were at identifying and addressing any risks and shortfalls. We looked at the governance framework to see whether this provided assurance to the Board. We also looked at what this meant at the ward and departmental level from the staff and patient perspective. We were assisted by a professional with board governance experience....

...General performance and clinical practice issues were dealt with at a range of committees which then reported to the Quality and Safety Committee then through the Governance Committee to the Trust

Board. We found reference to outstanding risks discussed at various committees but it was not clear what action was taken to address issues identified or timescales for actions. It is acknowledged that there were action logs for each committee meeting with timescales for actions recorded. We found that some issues such as access to safeguarding and mandatory training were raised at committee meetings over a period of months, yet no remedial action was evident to address the concerns.

We were particularly concerned about the fitness of the Operational Risk Register (dated July 2013). We found there were 719 risks identified in total, 388 had been on the risk register for over six months, with 217 rated as red risks (highest risk, with green as lowest.) We found that 265 risks did not have a risk rating (red, amber, green) and 509 risks did not have any action summaries, 163 of these were red rated. Many risks had missed their review date, some by six months or more. A high proportion had blank or incorrectly completed entries. This meant the Board could not be assured that once a risk had been identified that the appropriate actions were taken in a time appropriate manner and that problems with addressing any risks would be appropriately alerted to the Board.....

...A lack of engagement with clinical staff did not promote an environment where lessons learnt were always shared effectively. The trust management team told us they were aware of issues with engaging with clinicians and they were taking steps to engage better with clinical staff for example through the new "Listening Events" that had already taken place and would continue. A new medical director was due to start shortly and it was anticipated this would have a positive impact on relationships going forward.....

...We found that uptake of mandatory training was poor with only 56% completion against a target of

85%. We were particularly concerned that safeguarding issues may not be identified and action taken due to the low attendance at safeguarding training putting patients at risk. We were also concerned that the low numbers of staff completing Mental Capacity Act 2005 training meant a reliance of referrals to specific personnel and to another trust which could lead to unnecessary delays. Achievement against a target of 95% for staff appraisal was only 39%. It is acknowledged that there has been improvements in the numbers of medical staff being appraised. However, with poor uptake of mandatory training combined with a lack of appraisal, it would be difficult for the Board to be assured that the staff workforce were performing effectively."

The problem is this is not unique. There have been, in my view, too many scandals in both the UK and elsewhere, unyet they still occur. In the UK, the most recent scandal has been at the Mid-Staffordshire NHS Foundation Trust regarding high mortality rates. An initial investigation resulted in further examination of what was happening at the trust. Allegations arose that between 400 and 1200 more patients had died between 2005 and 2008 than would otherwise be expected. Eventually the UK Government initiated a public inquiry. This resulted in a final report in 2013, making 290 recommendations. Questions arose regarding the need for greater openness, transparency and candour amongst hospital staff to ensure the safety of patients whilst in hospital and the extent to which the report and its 290 recommendations would actually deliver changes resulting in safe and effective care being provided within the hospital itself. There have been other such inquiries in the UK regarding major failings in the health services, one of the most significant being that at Bristol Royal Infirmary relating to the provision of paediatric services.

But why do these scandals occur? Surely there are

checks and balances in place to protect patients. Well, there are but they do not work.

As part of my recovery, I have tried to understand my head pains and exhaustion, why I am experiencing them and what I can do to better minimise the impact they have on my daily life. I have had to delve deep and wide for answers; this has been and is exhausting but ultimately rewarding to know that I am not the only person living this experience with bipolar disorder – there are many others on a similar journey – some willing to share their experiences for which I am truly grateful.

I have had to raise my lack of progress with the CEO of the hospital in which I am being treated, I have had to go to the head of my GP practice to be listened to and I have had to continuously ask - why I am in such pain? Is it that no-one understands bipolar disorder? Is it because no-one understands the medication? And if they don't understand, in what way are they qualified to treat patients experiencing such symptoms? Are we just a ball being bounced around on a roulette wheel?

Thankfully, after what has seemed an eternity, I have received an initial assessment for admission to a pain management clinic programme for those experiencing chronic pain. I have been told there is a long waiting list but I guess at least I am in "the system" with regard to seeking some way of easing the head pains I experience daily. I have also received an assessment regarding my neuro-psychological abilities. A fascinating experience which required three appointments due to the fact that it took over 90 minutes to take my initial history, followed by a second appointment during which the tests were so taxing; not only did the pain in my head become beyond unbearable but I was practically asleep through exhaustion at the table at which myself and the neuropsychologist were sitting. Thankfully I managed to complete all tests by the third appointment. And to the "neuropsych", thank for your patience and sense of humour in coping with my limited ability to function as a human being.

There have been two elephants in the room which I have not yet given much coverage: CT and MRI scans. I had a feeling of ongoing exasperation with the lack of understanding demonstrated by many of the clinicians I was seeing regarding the head pains and exhaustion I was experiencing. I wanted to understand what was happening inside my head and what I could do to better manage the daily pain and exhaustion. I felt that a CT or an MRI scan might offer some insight. One GP said to me, "Well I doubt it will show anything." The psychiatrists made no reference to either scan. Only by going to see a different GP did I hear the magic words, "Well that is one of the first things I would have arranged for a patient of mine." The other elephant, related to my exhaustion and energy levels, relates to my sleep. As I mentioned earlier in this tome, I was diagnosed with sleep apnea before I took off into the world of mania. I pondered whether I was still experiencing mild symptoms which could be affecting the quality and quantity of sleep I might be getting. Finally, after many months of waiting, I had my initial assessment and apparently the structure of my skull and the formation of my mouth make me a high risk. I am lined up for a sleep study. [I have since had the sleep study and whilst I have a mild form of sleep apnea – it is only borderline so I have concluded that that is not contributing to my ongoing condition.]

As part of my recovery, I have been living a bit of a dual existence. One minute I am a normally-functioning human being, the next I am a zombie, consumed with pain and exhaustion. Ultimately, do we not all lead multiple existences, one at home in front of our close family, one in front of relatives we tolerate to a degree, one in the work environment, one with our close friends and one with acquaintances? If we put these different people together in one room, would they all describe the same you, the same me, the same us?

Whilst rummaging around in various piles of papers I

had gathered to write this book, I found a few nuggets I feel I should include at this point in the journey. I have not mentioned to date a couple of additional strings I added to my bow about a decade ago, becoming a PRINCE2 Certified Project Manager and an EFQM Assessor (EFQM standing for European Foundation of Quality Management). The equivalent in Australia is the Australian Business Excellence Framework and they have put together what they call, "Twelve Principles of Business Excellence" and I list them below, tweaked a little under my artistic licence:

1. clear direction allows organisational alignment and a focus on the achievement of goals
2. mutually-agreed plans translate organisational direction into actions
3. understanding of what customers value, now and in the future, influences organisational direction, strategy and action
4. improvement should constantly contribute in the outcome, the system and its associated processes
5. potential is realised through people's enthusiasm, resourcefulness and participation
6. continual improvement and innovation depends on continual learning
7. every individual lives and works in a system, outcomes can only be improved when people work together to improve that system
8. effective use of facts, data and knowledge results in improved decisions
9. all systems and processes exhibit variability, which impacts on predictability and performance
10. individuals that provide value to their community through their actions to ensure clean, safe, fair and prosperous society are more likely to lead rewarding lives
11. sustainability is determined by an individual's ability to create value for all their stakeholders
12. constant role modelling of the above principles

and their creation of a supportive environment in which to lives these principles are vital if the individual is to reach their true potential

All pretty laudable principles methinks, unyet given such little consideration as we glide through everyday life. I guess the challenge is that we are given a blank page at the beginning of our journey and it can be a fairly random journey along the way. Factors such as place of birth, upbringing, personality, schooling, DNA, motivation and chance/ luck all contribute to our journey. However, we ultimately steer our own ship. As I suggested in a previous chapter, you have to take control even when you are not in control. But why don't we? Why do we neglect our diet, neglect our bodies and our minds and what they are telling us? I ignored all the signs, I guess to be honest I did not understand my brain and I guess neither did my GP nor my psychologist. But if we do not understand our bodies and our minds, how can we make the most of what we have? After all, surely you would wish to live your life to its full potential, wouldn't you?

Whilst writing this book, dementia suddenly became a topic much talked about by politicians in the UK, Australia and elsewhere. This is an area where many health services should really look at what they are doing and put themselves in the shoes of those they are serving. To suggest paying a GP money to diagnose someone with a particular condition is wholly inappropriate but really raises to the fore, how prepared are those on the frontline to fully appreciate what it is like to be living a life with a condition that has such a debilitating impact on one's humanity as to be experiencing a mental condition and have no-one to reach out to, no-one to reassure, no-one to support and say "we are here for you and we will help you get through this as best we can"?

Moreover there is a lot that we, as individuals, can do to ensure we maximise our health and wellbeing. I found that the more I read and understand how the mind and body interacts and relies upon each other, the more I am able to maximise my ability to invest in myself through good diet, exercise and even more basic practices such as properly breathing (so much evidence that our shortened breathing patterns limit the amount of oxygen our body and brains so deeply rely upon) and mindfulness (the practice of meditation, emptying the mind and giving it some space to breathe).

Chapter 7
Take control – and here's how you can do it

Throughout my life, prior to my rollercoaster ride with bipolar disorder, I guess I have been fairly lucky to be in the right place at the right time. There have been, however a number of occasions where I have just ended up saying (to myself) WTF!

You may be aware of the wide variety of self-help/ find yourself/ find someone else to help you find yourself books available and the various fields of counselling, psychology and other fields of "medicine" that provide an opportunity to explore, understand and interpret what happened, why it happened and what one should do as a result of what happened kind of scenarios.

Ultimately, it is about taking control. And this I had to do even when I was not in control of either my mind or my body.

One of the most significant contributions to my recovery has been the field of neuro-linguistic programming. Whilst the term itself may result in many feeling tempted to put the kettle on or reach for the TV remote, it is – for me – one of the most powerful game-changers currently available to help guide us through the wonderful web of life.

To introduce it from its inception, Dr Richard Bandler (at the time a student psychologist), John Grinder (a linguistic professor) and Frank Pucelik got together to answer the following questions:

- How is it that some people excel at certain things when others don't?
- What makes them different and what is it that they are doing?

To explore how best to answer these questions, they focused on the work of three highly respected individuals

in their respective fields: Fritz Perls, Virginia Satir and Milton Erickson. These three individuals were widely acknowledged as being leaders in their field of effecting beneficial change in some of the most challenging of cases. Bandler, Grinder and Pucelik studied in detail every aspect of the work of these three individuals. This work resulted in a series of publications including:
- "The Structure of Magic";
- "The Structure of Magic II"
- "Frogs into Princes: Neuro-linguistic programming";
- "Using your brain for a change"
- "Reframing"

The work of Bandler, Grinder and Pucelik, broadly labelled "neuro-linguistic programming", helps in better understanding how our minds work, the source of our thoughts and behaviour and most importantly what we can do to change our thoughts and behaviour and subsequently improve the quality of our daily lives.

There have been many books written on NLP; you may have read one or two of them. I have enclosed a list at the back of the book detailing a few on my bookshelves.

Looking back across my journey, much of the content of NLP has contributed to my success without my consciously being aware of it. My wish as time progresses, is that NLP becomes ever more mainstream to the extent that those in their teenage years are introduced to the fascinating world that NLP opens up. Through employing NLP in those challenging but formative years, a deeper understanding can be achieved of who we are and what we seek to achieve in life which ultimately may contribute to a more strengthened foundation on which to build as life progresses.

The key aspects of NLP that I have found most useful are:
- our perception is our reality, no-one elses. Within our reality we each have different maps within which we function;

- our subconscious mind contains all the instruction booklets on which we draw in all our thoughts, decisions and actions;
- our values and beliefs can empower us or they can impede us;
- the meta programs;
- future pacing; and
- rapport.

Our perception is our reality, no-one else's – in order to understand the world, each of us subconsciously maps out what we consider our reality in our minds. In constructing these maps we do three things: delete, generalise and distort.

We delete information we do not think matters, information that does not align with our values or our view of our reality. We may delete information that could be important at a future date but, as we are living now, we decide to disregard it as irrelevant. For example, how many times do you get frustrated when going to the supermarket only to realise that items have been moved around and hence the map of your journey around the aisles to fulfil the purchase of the items on your shopping list is disrupted? You no longer know where things are, whereas you previously had an established map of the supermarket and knew where things were located and where you needed to go to get what was on your shopping list.

Have you ever taken a regular route from A to B and suddenly noticed something you had not before. Maybe a house, a junction or a building that you had not noticed before but suddenly bears some significance to you at that very moment in time. Have you ever gone into auto-pilot on a journey into work, allowing your eyes to drift across the passing scenery as time moves on? Generalisation is a key part of how the brain works. Put your hand on something hot, memory formed (note to self – avoid doing that again!) However the mind also adopts a similar approach when dealing with other life events such as break-ups, connections, arguments and the like. Your brain generalises all such memories and refers to them again, as and when it considers the need arises. This may or may not be a good thing. However in essence, the greater awareness we have of how our brain uses such ways of thinking, the more we can be conscious of our reasoning and how it affect the decisions and actions that influence our daily lives.

The brain also has a habit of distorting what we see, hear and do. It focuses on specific areas and ignores others resulting in a disproportionate representation of what we perceive to be reality. Do we end up feeling that the weather is always cold, the trains are always late, our bosses are always against us or the shops never stock what we need to feed ourselves? Sound familiar? Another more subtle distortion that occurs in our brain is the attachment of meaning to events, or to something someone says or does. There is an argument that suggests that in a conversation there are three realities: yours, that of the other person also in the conversation and a third arising from someone who may be looking and listening in to the conversation. How many times have you thought when reflecting on a past conversation, why didn't they understand what I'm saying? What were they looking at whilst I was talking to them? What was that conversation all about, we seemed to be talking about two completely different issues?

Deletions, Generalisations and Distortions are the reason behind many arguments. However, the more we expand our maps, explore others' maps or perhaps even be so bold as to identify areas of commonality in our respective maps – then the gaps can be identified, misunderstandings clarified and common ground built upon. And that is the power of NLP.

Our subconscious mind contains all the instruction booklets on which we draw - I call them instruction booklets for illustration purposes. In NLP they are known as strategies. Within our brains, we have strategies established for all the needs and wants that have arisen in our past. So, for example, in the morning we have a set of strategies for getting out of bed and ready for the day ahead. Our brain draws on sequences of finely-tuned strategies that enable us to get from "just woken up" to "fully showered, refreshed and ready." The challenge is to understand how our brain develops these strategies and to explore which of the strategies we have developed are serving us constructively and which are not.

Explore your own strategies on the following topics and reflect on whether they are adding value to your life or perhaps working against you in some way:

- allowing sufficient quality and quantity of sleep;
- pursuing a balanced approach to diet and exercise;
- goal-setting yearly, monthly, weekly and daily to provide focus and minimise distraction;
- diarising, enabling reflection on achievements, sense of direction and emptying of the mind on a regular basis to allow new beneficial feelings and thoughts to enter.

Now here is a quick strategy to try out when dealing with potentially stressful situations:

1. Recall a time when you were totally confident in dealing with someone you admired/respected/liked a lot;
2. Recall a specific time this occurred;
3. Go back to that time and full experience all the memories surrounding it;
4. As you remember it:
    - what was the very first thing that caused you to be totally confident and stress-free?
    - was it something you saw?
    - was it something you heard?
    - was it something you felt?
    - was it that it just felt the right thing to do?

5. What was the next thing that happened as you were totally confident and stress-free in that moment?
6. After you saw, heard or felt that, did you know you were totally confident and stress-free, did you picture something, say something? Or have a feeling? Did you have the end goal in sight? A clear objective associated with the action?
7. What contributed to the success of your interaction? Was the success driven by you? Someone else? Or was it a joint collaboration? A team effort?
8. Could this approach be replicated again and again?
9. Any key learnings? Could this transform how you approach certain issues in like and result in a more stress-free journey day in day out?

The key thing to remember here is that everything we decide, say and do consists of a series of strategies, stages or filters which our brain uses to guide us through the maze of life. These strategies, stages or filters are primarily drawn from our memories. That is how our behaviour is formed. That is called "growing-up". This does not mean we cannot change our strategies. We are totally empowered to change how we feel, think, say and do. Ultimately if we are truly present, we can also influence our gut instinct – something that often gets totally over-looked in life. The more we can draw on our gut instinct – called it intuition – the more authentic we can be in our daily lives.

Our values and beliefs can empower us or they can impede us – these aspects of our lives underpin so much of how we live life yet we may not be even aware of what our values and beliefs are. When was the last time someone asked you what you valued most in life? Have you ever been asked what you believe you are capable of in terms of potential achievement? We develop beliefs as we develop from childhood through teenage years into adulthood.

These beliefs can be influenced by those around us – family, relatives, school, friends, the communities in which we live, even the countries in which we live can have some influence on the beliefs we hold.

Values are more inherent and act like a compass to guide us in how to live our lives. Whilst these values may also be formed to some extent in a similar pattern to our beliefs, our values are considered more intrinsic to who we are as an individual and form a deeper part of our personality. It is possible to change values as a result of change in beliefs and vice versa, this can often occur through life experiences either of ourselves or those around us or both.

Values someone might associate with could include:
- acceptance
- achievement
- appreciation
- balance
- benevolance
- bravery
- cleanliness
- compassionate
- co-operation

Meta programs – this element of NLP covers a variety of perspectives on which our brains draw when making decisions. Our thinking can be summarised within the following frames of references:
- we are moving "towards pleasure" or "away from pain";
- we focus on our "internal" world or our "external" world;
- we prioritise "self" or "other";
- we prefer "options" or "procedures"
- we feel most comfortable conforming to the majority or gain most satisfaction from being different from others.

Chunking is another aspect of the meta model within which the brain functions. You can either chunk up, chunk down or chunk sideways. Chunking up is employed through asking, "for what purpose?" usually at most five times. So, for example, if you feel the need to confront someone about something, ask yourself, "for what purpose?" five times. If after this, you have arrived at a point where you see, hear or feel contentment and benefit created then you may consider a beneficial course of action has been identified. If you are unable, however to provide answers or find that the answers that emerge take you down a path that might be somewhat undesirable, then maybe the course of action might not be worth pursuing. Chunking down is applied through enquiring "what does this mean?", "all the time?" and "for example? And other examples?" - these questions assist in opening up more fully the map to determine the extent to which the map is actually the territory.

Chunking down is a classic technique applied when exploring perspective. For example you may feel that you are constantly stressed/ tired/ over-worked. But then ask yourself – is this occurring all time or only during specific times in the week or certain months of the year? This helps provide a little balance to the reality that you are creating for yourself.

Another way of using chunking is when confronted with a big decision to make – ask yourself – for what purpose do I need to make this decision? And once you have the answer, ask yourself again replacing the answer into the question – I outline how this might work with regard to purchase of a car:

- I want to buy a car but am not sure whether to buy car A or car B or whether I actually need to buy a car right now or whether I should delay the purchase.
- FOR WHAT PURPOSE... do you need to purchase a car right now?

- Because it will help me get about easier, I need to spend less time waiting for public transport and carrying heavy items around with me
- FOR WHAT PURPOSE do you need to spend less time waiting?
- Because I need to allocate more time to priorities in my life with which I need to make quicker progress?
- FOR WHAT PURPOSE do you need to allocate more time to priorities in your life to make quicker progress?
- Because then I can progress the growth within my business more efficiently and effectively, spend more time with people that matter to me and enjoy life more.
- Etc...

Future pacing – relates the now to the future – so, for example, if you have a decision you have to make, take yourself forward 6 months, 12 months, 5 years and then look back to the now and consider what would be the best option to choose. Another way of using future pacing is when presented with a challenging – or rather what may seem or feel like a challenging situation at the time and then future pace forward and reflect – will I remember this moment in five years' time? Will it affect my journey? My overall life? And then consider whether it is worth investing time and energy in that moment. After all, time moves on and if used to no effect could be considered wasted, the same could be applied to the energy we expend in the feeling, thinking and doing in every living moment.

Rapport – relates to the depth of connection, the relationship between two people. Through mirroring and matching an individual's behaviour and communication style, it is possible to deepen the level of rapport enabling trust and openness to strengthen. Mirroring and matching is in effect, mirroring and matching an individual's body movements and style of communication. Aspects such as tone and pace of voice, posture including head movements, hand gestures and crossing and uncrossing legs can enhance the level of rapport you have with someone. The key though in successfully implementing this approach is to do it subconsciously so that neither you nor the other person is actually consciously aware of what is happening – otherwise they may feel offended or think you are perhaps "trying it on"!

Moreover as well as mirroring and matching body language, it is possible to strengthen rapport through identifying and employing the same language as the other person with whom you are in conversation. We have five senses: sight, sound, feelings/ touch, smell and taste. In NLP, these senses are referred to as representational systems. Each individual has a preferred representational system – some people are more visual, some more auditory, some more kinesthetic.

Visual people are more likely to use language such as, I see what you mean, prefer to focus on colour and like living in a tidy home. They may be more susceptible to colourful clothes and surroundings and prefer to have new ideas explained through drawings or through imagery.

Auditory people include those who will be using language such as, I hear you, could you talk me through that again, have a large music collection and be very uncomfortable in silence.

Kinesthetic people use language such as "that feels about right", "that sits well with me" or "I grasp what you are on about". They are likely to be into textures, like warmth or coolness and be more focused on how they feel about something when making decisions.

Auditory – Digital people are those who are constantly seeking validation, certainty and evidence. They need things to be right, perfect, exact, spot on – nothing less will do. They will constantly be asking questions, looking for gaps and exploring different angles to determine the strength of anything put before them.

Neuroplasticity – we ARE in control!

The evidence is ever-increasing that our brains are constantly evolving with each minute we are alive. New memories are made, new patterns of behaviour are formed and new connections are made in our conscious and subconscious relating the now to the past which will be drawn on in the future whether we like it or not as a basis on which we form feelings and make decisions which we subsequently act upon as we progress through life. Why do we do what we do? Well if you truly wish to explore your "matrix" you can. You can either try out one of the many different personality models (such as Myers-Briggs, Birkman Method or DISC) or map out your life story identifying key events, key milestones and try to link all the various memories of everything that contributed to each of those little nuggets of your history that are now contributing one way or another to your present and your future to the way you are currently living your life.

Norman Doidge's book, entitled *The Brain that changes itself: stories of personal triumph from the frontiers of brain science* is one of the first game-changers in the field of neuro-plasticity in that it was able to catch the attention of mainstream media by portraying a series a personal stories of individuals who had, in effect, changed their brain. In each of the stories, details are provided as to how an individual's brain has adapted to deal with gaps or disconnections in the brains wiring. The brain had somehow put in place its own "work-around".

Barbara Arrowsmith-Young is another pioneer in this field. She authored the book, *The Woman who Changed her Brain*, describing her own journey from someone who read and wrote everything backwards, had trouble processing concepts in language, continuously got lost and was physically uncoordinated, through to eventually becoming someone who could read and write from left to right and become, ultimately, a normally functioning human being. Having seen this lady give a talk about her journey, I felt deeply moved by the determination that she, I guess myself and others display in grappling with something that so many know so little about. Unyet without our sheer desire to be human, we would probably be dead.

Baroness Susan Greenfield is another fascinating individual who has written extensively about the human brain. Her focus has been on researching brain physiology and the impact of Parkinson's and Alzeihmer's diseases on the way brains function. Her books include:
- Journey's to the centres of the Mind: Towards a science of consciousness (1995)
- The Human Brain: a Guided Tour (1997)
- The Private Life of the Brain (2002)
- Tomorrow's people: How 21st century technology is changing the way we think and feel (2003)
- Inside the body (2006)
- ID: The quest for identity in the 21st century
- You and Me: The Neuroscience of Identity (2011)

It's all in our DNA, or is it?

Taking a step deeper into who we are and what we want to achieve in our lives, I have become more and more intrigued about the role our DNA plays in influencing how we live our lives.

During my journey in exploring as much as I can about bipolar disorder and what I can do to minimise the risk of another episode of either depression or psychosis, I found there was a plethora of evidence showing that the condition is inherited. As I think I already have mentioned in an earlier chapter, I suspect both my father and his mother demonstrated symptoms that might suggest they also grappled with this aspect of their lives, though to my knowledge there was no formal diagnosis for either of them.

I was intrigued to explore the extent to which we are the result of our DNA or whether there is more to the balance of nature versus nurture. It is here that I hand over to a selection of the leading lights in the field.

David Goldman in his book, "Our genes, our choices: how genotype and gene interactions affect behaviour" (published 2012), noted that gene variations could predict differences in behaviour and indicate possible susceptibility to certain mental illness such as depression or psychosis. He refers to genetic predispositions to resilient "warrior" or cognitively advantaged "worriers" and also the significance of neuroplasticity of the brain and of our genes in that they are both constantly evolving, as part of a systematic growth and feedback loop of learning that is in constant adjustment and refinement. He concludes his book by noting "We are only at the beginning of this journey, and not too near the end of the beginning, to understand how a restricted set of genes can program the rules by which the brain develops, and the implications of stochasticity and decision making in the development of human individuality. However, we already know well enough that we are all neurogenetically individual and that we are all free."

In their book *Living with our genes: why they matter more than you think*, published in 1998, Dean Hamer and Peter Copeland suggest that despite the risks of trying to reduce what genes will do, there are ways to benefit from understanding our genetic makeup. They suggest that, as it might be considered commonsense to not follow patterns of behaviour that may pre-exist in the family environment such as over-consumption of alcohol or calories, they note that the only difference with genes relating to personality and behaviour is that the effects are more subtle and still less understood.

"When you think about the genes for your own personality, you are asking, "who am I?" The simple answer is, "you are who your brain thinks you are." And who your brain thinks you are is the result of an intricate, one-of-a-kind interaction of genes and life experiences."

Finally, in his book *The genius of all of us* (published 2010), David Shenk concludes that:
- no one is born with a predetermined amount of intelligence. Intelligence can be improved;
- few adults come close to their true intellectual potential;
- like intelligence, talents are not innate gifts, but the result of a slow, invisible accretion of skills developed from the moment of conception;
- everyone is born with differences, and some with unique advantages for certain tasks. But no one is genetically designed into greatness and few are biologically restricted from attaining it;
- the old nature/ nurture paradigm suggests that control over our lives is divided between genes (nature) and our own decision (nurture). In fact, we have more control over our genes and far less control over our environment than we think;
- it must not be left to our genes and parents to foster greatness; spurring individual achievement is also the duty of society. Every culture must strive to foster values that bring out the best in its people;
- everything we know about epigenetics so far fits perfectly with the dynamic systems model of human ability. Genes do not dictate what we are to become, but instead are actors in a dynamic process. Genetic expression is modulated by outside forces. "Inheritance" comes in many forms: we inherit stable genes, but also alterable epigenetics; we inherit languages, ideas, attitudes, but can also change them. We inherit ecosystem, but can also change it;
- everything shapes us and everything can be shaped by us. The genius in all of us is our built-in ability

to improve ourselves and our world.

Me and my magic carpet

I have encountered times when my brain is totally in flow and I have been able to deal with everything and anything. There have been other times when my brain has been in such pain and exhaustion that I can do nothing but lie down and rest, often resulting in my falling asleep for 2-3 hours. Oh the joys of bipolar medication.

When I experience moments of exasperation, I hop on my magic carpet and either travel to a moment in my past to draw on a state of being which will help my mental and physical state or to a moment in the future where I see myself being what I want to be, where I want to be, with people I want to be with. This really intrigues me as in the past I would have found myself becoming angry, frustrated, exhausted and generally fed-up. However now I just sit back and away I go on my little trip. And what a difference it makes to my physiology.

I was pondering how I could explain this sort of disassociation in more detail and came up with the text below:

"Sit still in a quiet place where you will not be disturbed. Place your hands gently on your thighs and your feet naturally on the ground. Allow your breathing to slow and your body to relax. With every breath you are feeling more and more relaxed. And gently close your eyes. [this may be something to record and subsequently play back to yourself to complete the exercise.] And as you drift into a state of deep relaxation, imagine yourself floating up above a timeline of your life and looking down on your past, present and future.

Now as you look at your past, you see all those times whether good or bad, the experiences you enjoyed and those from which you learnt, the life changing moments, the exhilarating highs and the exasperating barriers you overcame. Each moment of your past has contributed to your foundation, to your here and now, to your success as you journey forward. Notice the useful information, the clues and the signs floating up out of each of those experiences like a flotilla of balloons, floating above your timeline and supporting you as your progress forward and leave your past behind.

Then imagine yourself as all of these balloons float further upwards, the sky becomes floodlit like the floodlights at a stadium and you are onstage with your audience before you, cheering you on as you glide from success to success. Soak up the energy, soak up the adulation from your audience, feel energised and embrace openly all that you are being offered. Then take this energy, this adulation and scatter gently this effect along your timeline from here to the point you entered the world and back again.

Now look back on your past as you notice the energy and adulation coat your past in a new perspective, a new realisation that the past is past and your future awaits your taking your first steps forward.

And now as you float back into yourself in the new reality full of energy and adulation – new people, new successes and new worlds await. The world is at your feet!

Enjoy"

Ultimately what truly matters, I guess is being happy, motivated and calm. As the famous saying goes, "Keep calm and carry on". Ironically, I found the text below on my iPad, whilst writing this chapter – again written when I was psychotic. And again, so insightful – it makes me think there is more to psychosis and how the brain operates in this state than anyone has really truly explored.

"calm:
- calm allows the mind to function at its best - and it encourages rational and empathetic thinking. This allows planning, decision-making and focused thinking, without being

distracted. calm enables balanced judgement;
- calm is the mood for reading, studying, meditating, praying, listening to music, walking in the country and being at one with nature. it is the mood for successful negotiation, where both sides are heard equally. a calm mood helps in making sound decisions in the present, developing plans for the future and in learning lessons from the past. being calm is about being at ease with yourself and who you are;
- calm communication is clear and unrushed - enabling understanding whilst carry authority.
- calm is all too often neglected in modern life - it allows you to be happy, it offers a deeper understanding and appreciation. calm offers contemplation - of nature, the kindness of friends and the beauty of life;
- calm people are happy, peaceful people who make us feel good when they are around. calm is a mood at ease with itself and with the world, it is gentle and quiet, it is a place of intimacy, of relaxation and healing. calms forms the platform of self-management. Being assertive is about learning to be calm in the face of authority, threat or fear;
- calm people are serene, unhurried, deliberate and economical. They are untroubled and possess a sense of peace and stability. They set their own peace regardless of what is happening around them. The calm efficiency of a well-grounded person is easily recognized;
- calmness is cool-headedness - leadership is the ability to stay calm under fire, while taking responsibility and making objective and effective decisions;
- a calm life is one that contains trust, security and faith in the future - it represents the belief

that all will work out for the best in the end - and that whatever happens - it is for the best.

Annex A

The Lime Green Solutions
offering calmer coaching
–
for a better life!

My Personal Wellbeing Plan

My vision for me:

My mission for me:

My values which empower me to achieve my mission and support my vision:

Desired Outcome:

Desired Outputs:

Desired Process:

Desired Inputs:

Desired Environment:

Why should I bother?

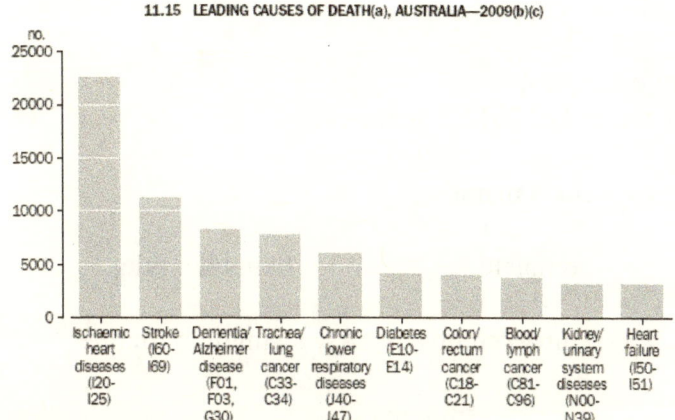

11.15 LEADING CAUSES OF DEATH(a), AUSTRALIA—2009(b)(c)

(a) Causes listed are the leading causes of death for all deaths registered in 2009, based on WHO recommended tabulation of leading causes.
(b) Causes of death data for 2009 are preliminary and subject to a revisions process.
(c) See Explanatory Notes of Causes of Death, Australia, 2009 (3303.0) for further information on specific issues relating to 2009 data.

Source: ABS data available on request, Causes of Death, Australia, 2009.

The Top causes of death in Australia in 2012 were:

And lifespan...

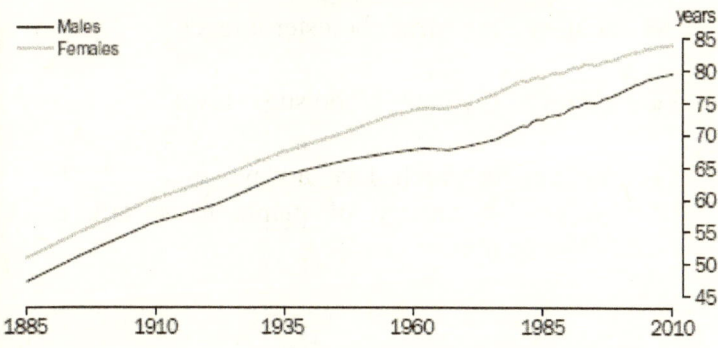

11.16 LIFE EXPECTANCY AT BIRTH—1885–2010

Source: ABS data available on request, Australian Historical Population Statistics, 2008; Deaths, Australia, 2009.

So to avoid a possible causes of death and maximise my lifespan I plan to: ………………..
[SMART Targets – Specific, Measurable, achievable, Realistic, Timely]

For example:
By the end of 2014, I will have:

- run a marathon,

- completed at least one 10km bike ride,

- embarked on a weekly swimming routine,

- given up smoking

- be eating five veggie servings and three of fruit each day

- achieved my ideal weight

- achieved my ideal blood pressure

- achieved my ideal cholesterol level

- achieved my ideal blood sugar level

- the veggie patch I've always dreamed of, growing a variety of plants to sustain a balanced diet

MY TARGETS
for the period ____ / ____ / ____ to ____ / ____ / ____
are:

1.

2.

3.

4.

5.

6.

7.

8.

9.

10.

Sixteen tips to improve your lifestyle

(adapted from 77 ways to improve your wellbeing – how to use Ancient Chinese Wisdom to enhance your physical, mental and spiritual health by Angela Hicks)

Please detail below the achievements you personally plan to deliver for each of these tips…

Tip no 1: four important stages of integrating lifestyle changes

Tip no 2: refine your intention

Tip no 3: know what's stopping you

Tip no 4: prepare to enhance your lifestyle

Tip no 5: Put your lifestyle plan into action

Tip no 6: Completion and integration – make a new adjustment into a regular habit

Tip no 7: Find ways to become motivated

Tip no 8: Make your goals specific and achievable

Tip no 9: Allow yourself some imperfections

Tip no 10: Take teeny tiny steps (in the right direction)

Tip no 11: Do what you find enjoyable

Tip no 12: Find healthy substitutes

Tip no 13: Change at your own speed

Tip no 14: It takes a month to change a habit

Tip no 15: See yourself changing your lifestyle, hear what you are saying, feel what you are feeling

Tip no 16: Don't just read about it – use it, do it!

Connect with us...
F: The Lime Green Solutions
T: @davevirgo
W: www.calmercoaching.com

Further gems can be found in....

- 77 ways to improve your wellbeing – how to use Ancient Chinese Wisdom to enhance your physical, mental and spiritual health by Angela Hicks
- A path to happiness: a guide to living a balanced life by Dalai Lama
- Brain Bugs: How the Brain's Flaws Shape Our Lives by Buonomano, Dean
- Dark Nights Of The Soul: A guide to finding your way by Thomas Moore
- Finding Your Way in a Wild New World: Reclaim Your True by Martha Beck
- How to Create a Mind: The Secret of Human Thought Revealed by Ray Kurzweil
- Keep Your Brain Alive-83 Neurobic Exercises to Help Prevent Memory by Lawrence Katz
- Life without Limits by Nick Vujicic
- Living On Your Own Terms by Osho
- No Excuses: The Power of Self-Discipline by Brian Tracy
- Success Against the Odds by Brett Wigdortz
- The 8 Traits Successful People Have in Common: 8 to Be Great by Richard St John
- The 21st Century Brain: Explaining, Mending and Manipulating the Mind by Steven Rose
- The Answer by Glenn Harrold
- The Case Against Perfection by Michael J. Sandel
- The Gifts of Imperfection by Brené Brown
- The Happiness Myth: Why What We Think Is Right Is by Jennifer Hecht
- The Human Mind Explained: The Control Centre of The Living Machine by Susan Greenfield
- Way of the Peaceful Warrior by Dan Millman
- When Everything Changes, Change Everything by Neale Donald Walsch
- Your Soul's Gift by Robert Schwartz

Annex B
Meetup e-mails

5/4/14 3:55 PM

Hi there,
How are you?

Well after a month in the UK I am back in wonderful Melbourne and gosh the weather has changed. And so to the theme of this e-mail - change. I can certainly speak from experience here - having gone from a living a fairly routine 9 to 5 existence to one of extreme highs and extremes low caused apparently - and now officially - by a bipolar brain. And so now I am in the process of changing how I think, how I feel and how I live my life. It is just how life is. I have been there done that and I'd now like to begin a new chapter which I feel is now evolving.

I was in the UK to see my elderly mother - 87 years old - she is my superstar. Sadly her health is not so good and I have found a yet another new chapter revealed for which I have previously had no preparation - old age. I was lucky to catch a programme on the BBC - if you have iPlayer on iPad you may be able to watch the programme, it is wonderfully structured and has some delightful personal stories. What really struck me though it the most powerful message - we are not alone, we are all in many ways following a similar to those before and alongside us (though we may be not be aware of this at the time) and we all have questions which others have and are seeking answers to. Sometimes there are no answers, sometimes it is ideal just to accept what is, take a deep breath and thank yourself for being you and achieving what you have achieved - however big or small you may feel that may be - self-gratitude is a huge trait as

well as compassion and kindness - thanking yourself for being you and all that you, all that you have been and all that you can be is BIG - go on treat yourself!
Enjoy,
Dave.

P.S. If you are like affirmations, I post daily on facebook at https://www.facebook.... and on twitter at @davevirgo.

3/31/14 7:28 PM

Hi there,
 Are you in pain?
 Have you asked anyone for help?
 Did they respond in a helpful manner?
 I have been raised the issue of head pain with my GP and psychiatrist for a while now. Thankfully I have now been referred to the Caulfield Pain Management Clinic via my GP - this has opened doors to new awareness including a better understanding of what the pain is that I am experiencing and what I can do to manage it better/minimise its impact on my daily life.

Thought I might share a few links:
neuromatrix - the source of all pain?
http://www.specialist...
Chronic Pain Australia
www.chronicpainaustralia.org
Pain Tool Kit
www.paintoolkit.org
Hunter Valley Pain Service -video of cartoon explaining pain
http://youtu.be/4b8oB...

3/18/14 9:21 AM

Hello,

So much happening in the outside world, it got me even more interested in our DNA and the extent to which we are aware of the impact that the outside world has on our DNA. There is ever increasing evidence that our DNA is constantly evolving and there is much evidence that our beings are in constant renewal - the question is - are we allowing this change to evolve, are we steering changes within us or are we focused within and without and hence able to evolve into fully conscious beings? For example - repeat the following ten times each morning before you start the day and notice any changes to how you feel - the phrase - "I am awesome and on my journey to superstardom".

Enjoy, Dave C.

The past is the past - but it can be a gift to invest in our futures...
http://tinybuddha.com...
Have you already all the answers you need?
http://selfavenue.com...
We all have choices, channels through which we invest energy...
http://selfavenue.com...
Do you feel fully refreshed in the morning? Here's a way to get a good nights sleep...
http://healthyhints.c...
Something a little different but hey we all want to look awesome...
http://healthyhints.c...

3/8/14 10:14 AM

Hi there,

Hope you are well.

I thought I might focus on health - your health. Sometimes we can be so focused on one part of being, we forget the rest is there too and might need a little TLC. Moreover, the importance of sleep is increasingly being recognised so I felt you may be interested in the contents and links below (the sleep links are at the bottom of the e-mail) - it always nice to know how you're travelling - enjoy, Dave C.

From wisebread.com...
"The 6 Most Important Health Appointments You Must Stop Avoiding
Posted: 07 Mar 2014 02:48 AM PST

Between work, family, and every other personal obligation, you might forget to take good care of yourself. Too many unhealthy foods may creep into your diet; workouts might become few and far between; and doctor visits might be the furthest thing from your mind — at least until you start to feel sick. (See also: How to Feel Better Fast)

However, the time to think about your health isn't after you suspect a problem. Just about every medical condition has an early stage, and an early diagnosis can be the key to long-term health and longevity. Not that you should obsess about healthcare or schedule needless doctor visits; but there are appointments that you should make every year.

1. Annual Wellness Checkup or Physical

There is no hard and fast rule regarding how often we should get an annual physical. Some in the medical field suggest yearly checkups for everyone, yet others feel that annual physicals aren't necessary until the age of 50.

But even if your doctor says that you can go two or three years between physicals, there is no harm in an annual trip. Our health can change quickly and a physical exam can possibly detect hidden illnesses before symptoms develop.

For example, your doctor will listen to your heartbeat during the physical, and any irregular sounds might suggest a heart murmur or another cardiac issue. He'll also check your blood pressure and order a series of blood tests which can evaluate blood sugar and cholesterol levels, and determine whether your organs are functioning properly. (See also: Natural Ways to Lower Your Blood Sugar)

Additionally, annual physicals conducted by a primary physician can include gender-specific examinations, such as a clinical breast exam, a Pap smear, and a pelvic exam for women, and a testicular exam for men. This is also your chance to discuss any issues or concerns with your doctor.

2. Eye Exam

If your vision is perfectly clear and you don't have any eye problems, you can probably schedule an eye exam every two to four years. However, if you wear corrective lenses, have a known eye problem, or a history of diabetes or high blood pressure, yearly examinations are important for keeping your prescription up-to-date and assessing the health of your eyes.

Some eye diseases that cause complete vision loss are treatable if caught early. For example, with an early diagnosis your doctor may be able to slow the progression of age-related macular degeneration and perhaps reverse vision loss. The same is true for glaucoma, which is the leading cause of blindness in the United States. The longer it takes to diagnose an eye disease, the greater the risk for permanent damage.

3. Skin Exam

A survey conducted by the Skin Cancer Foundation found that 42% of those polled received asunburn at least once a year. And since it only takes "one blistering sunburn in childhood or adolescence to double a person's chances of developing melanoma later in life," annual skin exams by a dermatologist are crucial for diagnosing melanoma and non-melanoma skin cancers early. (See also: 7 Ways to Protect Your Skin)

And don't think you're safe just because you've never experienced sunburn. There is still a risk if you have a family history of skin cancer, or if you have several sizable moles on your body.

During the appointment, your dermatologist will examine your body from head to toe and check for suspicious moles — and if necessary, remove and biopsy questionable skin marks.

Although the majority of moles are harmless, you shouldn't hesitate to make an appointment with your dermatologist if you're worried about a skin spot, or if a mole changes in size or appearance.

4. Dental X-Rays

Dental cleanings every six months contribute to your oral health. But in addition to regular cleanings, you should schedule dental X-rays about every one to three years, depending on the overall health of your teeth and age. (See also: How to Avoid Expensive Dental Problems)

For example, adults and adolescents with a low risk for decay can go 18 to 36 months between X-rays, yet it's recommended that those with a higher risk for decay schedule annual X-rays.

Dental X-rays are painless and quick. They can help your doctor identify decay that's not visible from an oral examination, as well as reveal bone loss and other abnormalities.

5. Flu Vaccination

You might view the flu as nothing more than a severe cold, but it's much more. (See also: Frugal Ways to Treat a Cold)

This virus is responsible for nearly 36,000 deaths and 200,000 hospitalizations in the United States each year. And although flu-related complications are higher in young children, the elderly, pregnant women, and those with a compromised immune system, the virus can kill healthy adults as well.

The flu vaccine is recommended for everyone over the age of six months, and it offers 90% protection. Although a vaccination is optional, an annual shot can potentially save your life or the life of someone you love.

6. Mammogram

The recommendations for breast cancer screening vary, with some organizations like the National Cancer Institute advocating mammograms every one to two years starting at the age of 40.

Women in their 20s and 30s should have a clinical breast examination every one to three years by a primary care physician or gynecologist, reports Susan G. Komen."

Ten Health Benefits of a Good Night's Sleep - http://longevity.abou...
Better sleep guidelines - http://sleepdisorders...
How much sleep do I need? - http://sleepdisorders...
Overview of common sleep disorders - http://sleepdisorders...

3/2/14 6:21 PM

Hi there,

Time marches on eh? Please excuse the pun, there is much happening out there in the big wide world but for what purpose does it matter to us? You may read the news, you may engage with current affairs, catch up with your favourite magazine. And how does that make you feel? To what extent are you consciously or subconsciously engaging with what you see, hear, feel? Are you aware of the impact new information has on you? Are you aware of the impact old information has on you?

And so to the links. Enjoy, Dave C.

Memories – do they add value? are they a ball and chain? Or both?
http://tinybuddha.com...
Is your life an experience or a belonging?
http://www.themuse.co...
Your character influences your every moment, your every feeling, your every thought...
http://www.good.is/po...
You are an icon, a powerball, a leader of change for good – a nudge is the right direction can always help:
http://idiotsguides.c...

2/19/14 9:43 AM

Hi there,

How are you?

I went along to a really intriguing talk yesterday evening given by a local GP and senior psychologist of one of our hospitals. It's topic? "Coping with depression". Oh gosh, I thought, a must go to event. I left the event bemused. Why? Because, in the context of the material they presented, I felt more informed than them on the topic. The psychologist had an interest perspective informed on a rather traditional perspective of depression and he referred heavily to beyondblue and The Black Dog Institute. The GP, offered additional insight, focusing more the pharma approach to depression - bit of an eye-opener, especially the comment about Victoria being the "prescription state" of Australia, that is, Victoria is perceived at having a tendency to prescribe multiple medication simultaneously. My take on all this? Well I am a strong believe in neuroplasticity and the ability of each individual to transform their brains, their minds and their bodies and hence their whole life. Whilst these transformations may not happen instantaneously, the more time and energy invested in deeply reconnecting with feelings, thoughts and actions to uplift our spirit and draw us nearer to what "allows us to shine ever brighter", the greater will be our magnetic pull/ push towards our ultimate path and goal.

On a personal note, I have opened up a few more spots for my calmercoaching experience. If you would like to see what it's all about, hear more from me or feel the experience of being coached by someone who knows a thing or two about how to fulfil potential and enhance personal productivity, e-mail me back and we can go from there.

And so the links. Enjoy, Dave C.

You know what you want in life. Keep the focus and allow your new reality to come to fruition...
http://www.spring.org...
Accept, allow, achieve...
http://tinybuddha.com...
Flourish.... if you're heart allows...
http://www.brainpicki...
Extracted from the link above, you may wish to try out the two innovations below:

Innovation 1

"Close your eyes. Call up the face of someone still alive who years ago did something or said something that changed your life for the better. Someone who you never properly thanked; someone you could meet face-to-face next week. Got a face?

Gratitude can make your life happier and more satisfying. When we feel gratitude, we benefit from the pleasant memory of a positive event in our life. Also, when we express our gratitude to others, we strengthen our relationship with them. But sometimes our thank you is said so casually or quickly that it is nearly meaningless. In this exercise ... you will have the opportunity to experience what it is like to express your gratitude in a thoughtful, purposeful manner.

Your task is to write a letter of gratitude to this individual and deliver it in person. The letter should be concrete and about three hundred words: be specific about what she did for you and how it affected your life. Let her know what you are doing now, and mention how you often remember what she did. Make it sing! Once you have written the testimonial, call the person and tell her you'd like to visit her, but be vague about the purpose of the meeting; this exercise is much more fun when it is a surprise. When you meet her, take your time reading your letter."

Innovation 2

"Every night for the next week, set aside ten minutes

before you go to sleep. Write down three things that went well today and why they went well. You may use a journal or your computer to write about the events, but it is important that you have a physical record of what you wrote. The three things need not be earthshaking in importance ("My husband picked up my favorite ice cream for dessert on the way home from work today"), but they can be important ("My sister just gave birth to a healthy baby boy").

Next to each positive event, answer the question "Why did this happen?" For example, if you wrote that your husband picked up ice cream, write "because my husband is really thoughtful sometimes" or "because I remembered to call him from work and remind him to stop by the grocery store." Or if you wrote, "My sister just gave birth to a healthy baby boy," you might pick as the cause ... "She did everything right during her pregnancy."

Writing about why the positive events in your life happened may seem awkward at first, but please stick with it for one week. It will get easier."

2/15/14 8:55 PM

Hello,

My again - how are you?

I have to admit I have one of the most fun days with my lovely head - ended up most of the day asleep and now - at almost 9pm - am feeling "normal"ish - what joy eh?

You may have seen the recent movie - Frozen - there is a wonderful song in there entitled "Let it go" - have a peek at the link below - the song is quite a tune as are the lyrics quite wonderful...

http://www.youtube.co...

Well it is that time of the month again - our meetup is scheduled for next Saturday - 2pm at the Starbucks on Swanston near corner Swanston and Londsale - I should have the meetup sign on display at the big table on the raised area at the back of the coffee shop - look forward to seeing anyone/ everyone who is able to get along - if you can't no probs - there will always be another chance...

Enjoy :)
Dave C.

P.S I post all these e-mails on the message board forum - Interesting articles/ Useful links - new members may wish to peruse past e-mails and links - there are a few golden nuggets in there

P.P.S. I also post info on wellbeing/ wellness/ mental health on my facebook page -

https://www.facebook....

P.P.P.S. If you love a daily affirmation - I post in the morning at

https://www.facebook....

or if you are on twitter - please feel free to follow my tweets - @davevirgo

2/12/14 12:15 PM

Hi there,

Have you ever perceived yourself as a leader?

Have you ever been a leader?

Are you a leader now?

The reason I ask? Well I have been reading a fascinating book, A first-rate madness: uncovering the links between leadership and mental illness by Nassir Chaemi. In what way is it fascinating? Well it argues that some of the world's greatest leaders have achieved greatness through their journey with mental illness and that the manner in which they have channelled their journey with mental illness has been their greatest strength. Examples cited include Winston Churchill with his dogged determination to success no matter what, Abraham Lincoln with this empathy, tenaciousness and deep humanity enabling him to connect and empower a nation in times of adversity and Franklin Roosevelt whose ability to overcome obstacles in his life with an energy and spirit which became the hallmark of his presidency.

And so to the links, Enjoy, Dave C :)

Nudge or nuzzle...?
http://www.horizons.g...
Focus on lifting your heart and your life will follow...
http://tinybuddha.com...
Our buttons and our triggers...
http://keystothemind....
What does wellness/ wellbeing mean to you?
https://www.facebook....
...and an article which might be of interest....

The Power of Patience by Sharon Salzberg
If we can be quieter, more in the moment with what is

actually happening, a world of perception opens up for us based on where we are, not on where we one day hope to be. "Nobody sees a flower, really; it is so small," said artist Georgia O'Keeffe. "We haven't time, and to see takes time, like to have a friend takes time." If we learn to take a little more time and be more fully aware of just where we are, we might see many new flowers and have many more friends.

One way of describing an ability to hold our convictions without drawing premature conclusions, feeling automatically defeated, or losing sight of what goodness life might be offering us today is the old-fashioned virtue patience. Despite the common misconception, having patience doesn't mean making a pact with the devil of denial, ignoring our emotions and aspirations. It means being wholeheartedly engaged in the process that's unfolding, rather than yanking up our carrots, ripping open a budding flower, demanding a caterpillar hurry up and get that chrysalis stage over with.

True patience isn't gritting one's teeth and saying, "I'll bear with this for another five minutes because I'm sure it will be over by then and something better will come along." Patience isn't dour, and it isn't unhappy. It's a steady strength that we apply to each experience we face. If the situation calls for action, we must take it - patience doesn't mean inertia or complacence. Instead, it gives us a courageous dedication to the long haul, along with the willingness to connect with the multilayered truth of what is right here.

Are those of us not naturally blessed with patience doomed to yell at our children or our forgetful parents, litter our office floors with disemboweled computer parts (or at least threaten to), or berate ourselves each time we fail to live up to our own expectations? Or can we cultivate a new way of responding?

Anytime we're waiting - for the checkout person to ring us up, for the doctor's office to call, for a friend who has hurt us to apologize - we can remember we're alive right now. We can be determined to use this moment as a vehicle for paying attention, for growing, for opening.

Whenever we're pushing against what is, as though if we tried hard enough we could force the tempo of change, we can take a breath. Whatever our vision for how things should be in the future, we can make sure we do the very next thing we need to do today. And whenever we're in a fury of impatient resentment because our companion is walking too slowly or the mail came too late or we're being ignored or we can't concentrate or we can't name what we want - or any of the countless everyday things we find hard, we can remind ourselves of what is good right now. Then, as we work to redress what is wrong, the belligerence, agitation, and frustration will drain out of our "now," and the word can become a declaration of purpose and strength, supported by the gentle, developing power of patience.

2/11/14 12:38 PM

Hi there,

How are you?

What the question are you asking yourself today?

What is your primary goal today?

What is your ultimate outcome you want to achieve today?

The challenge is there is so much choice for each of us, the question is - what choice best serves us at this moment in time?

Ultimately answers are dependent on so many channels through which the question can be interpreted, information that can be used to guide the answer and ultimately, balancing our mind, body and soul to enable deep connection with our feelings to enable us to trust our intuition that supports us each and every day.

Here are a few links which may assist you on your journey - Enjoy, Dave C.

Evolve your brain...
http://www.youtube.co...
Empower your thoughts....
http://www.youtube.co...
Change your rules, change your thoughts, change your life...
http://www.youtube.co...
Meditation - ever more powerful to calm the mind and allow us space to be...
http://www.youtube.co...
Success or fulfilment - you choose...
http://www.youtube.co...

2/4/14 9:29 AM

Hi there,

How are you?

I write this e-mail in a moment of cool weather. How wonderful we live in a country of variety, one where one day it is cool and then next a little warmer and then a little warmer or a little cooler - no day is the same. And so in our lives, no day is the same. Whilst it contains the standard elements - waking, sleeping, eating, talking, pondering, thinking, feeling - we have the ability to influence our feelings, our thoughts our movements. With self-knowledge, we can live wonderful lives. The key here is self-knowledge.

Are we brought up with open minds?

Are we empowered to live each day to the best of our ability?

Are we able to connect with what makes our hearts soar?

Are we told that the power of our feelings, our thoughts, and our actions influences every second of every day and that this can greatly influence the outcome arising from that?

Self-acceptance can be the most empowering aspect of our journey. Sometimes, we may be able to glide through the day, other times they may be a few humps and bumps in the road before us. Life evolves, nature evolves, seasons change, the sun rises, the sun sets - we know the sun will rise again; we know the seasons will return - do we know what we happen to us tomorrow? More importantly, do we know what to do in response to what happens? And even more importantly, do we truly know what matters in our journey forwards? what is adding value each and every day and how we can guide ourselves each and every day to support ourselves evolve into the developing the deepest connections with ourselves, our friends and our world?

And so to the links. Enjoy, Dave C.

Living your best life:
http://blackdoctor.or...
Take a blank sheet of paper:
http://www.good.is/po...
Sleep helps refuel the mind, body and soul:
http://www.spring.org...
Follow the path of someone and model their experience, or lay out your own path:
http://www.independen...

1/23/14 12:18 PM

Hi there,
How are you?
Have you read the book *What colour is my parachute*? For $9.63 on Amazon Kindle - this book takes you on a journey, a journey of self-exploration, a journey through which you are invited to connect with your values, your motivations, and your burning desires.

I read the book and connected with my desire to be a coach, a life coach - naff you may think - but I love doing it, I am told I have a knack and I am looking forward to a time when I can and will fully engage with this path - check out my website at www.calmercoaching.com and click on the Facebook, Twitter or LinkedIn icons to find out more about me if you wish.

And so to the links - Enjoy - Dave C.

Taking action:
http://fatherhood.abo...
Impact of exercise on our mental health:
http://depression.abo...
The days are slowing shortening:
http://depression.abo...
It should not be so - but world over it is:
http://www.independen...
But we all have rights and there are standards:
http://health.vic.gov...
http://www.health.vic...

1/13/14 8:08 AM

Hello,

Is your hand on your steering wheel?

Interesting start to an e-mail?

I say this in the context of a fascinating day yesterday in which I prepared myself for the forthcoming warm period of weather, through purchase and construction of a fan from Officeworks – a nice cool breeze anticipated during those warmish evenings, a visit to the City Library to pick my latest reservations and then a visit to Midsumma to catch up the latest goings-on in one of the city's iconic events.

So what with the title? Well, Midsumma has a lot going on including lots of stalls with a variety of organisations presenting their wares. The one thing that bemused me was the challenge I experienced in trying to quickly connect with whether or not I should approach each stand. Whilst there was a lot of colour, people and activity, I frequently found it difficult to understand the purpose behind the stall - what did the stall offer? How would my life change through approaching the stall? What doors might open? What new connections might appear? Could there be some information that could inspire me in my daily life?

This got me thinking, rather amused as I was, well this was not the nature of the thoughts and feelings I was expecting to experience in visiting the event. And so the takeaway from all this - well I have found that in maintaining both the motivation, the energy and the focus on my recovery from the psychosis - I need to ensure my hand is constantly on the steering wheel of my feelings, my thoughts. I have to constantly check in to ensure I am ok, balance, stable. Cool - all makes sense? However, sometimes we could slightly loosen our grip on the steering wheel to allow new experiences into our lives and open up new horizons into how we perceive our reality. Sometimes we just have to take time out, lie on the ground and look up at the stars, for they are there for a purpose, they are there to uplift our souls, our hearts and engage our minds to the beauty in the world.

And so to a few links which I hope, if you get a chance to have a peek at, you find of some use - thank you and enjoy,
Dave C.

The power of a cup of coffee:
http://www.kindspring...
Green spaces enhance your mental health and wellbeing:
http://www.spring.org...
You can live out your dreams:
http://www.thedailymu...
Vulnerability invites kindness:
http://www.kindspring...
Living in the prescence allays anxiety:
http://www.brainpicki...
10 awe-inspiring studies into your mind:
http://www.spring.org...

Annex C

My bookshelves contain the following gems:

The future of the mind: the scientific quest to understand, enhance and empower the mind – Michio Kaku
Brainspotting – David Grand
We are our brains – Dick Schwab
Collapsing consciously – Carolyn Baker
The Tao of Bipolar – Anellen M Simpkins
Nudge: Improving decision about health, wealth and happiness – Richard H Thaler
Why isn't my brain working – Datis Kharrazian
mBraining: Using your multiple brains to do cool stuff – Grant Soosalu and Markin Oka
NLP: The essential guide – Tom Hoobyar, Tom Dotz and Susan Sanders
Innovations in NLP – L Michael Hall and Shelle Rose Charvet
Your many faces – Virginia Satir
Cracked: why psychiatry is doing more harm than good – James Davies
Brain change – David DiSalvo
The Compassionate Mind – Paul Gilbert
Focus – Daniel Goleman
When everything changes change everything – Neale Walsh
The Plastic Mind – Sharon Begley
The Neurotourist – Lone Frank
Life is what you make it – Ernest Holmes
Bipolar Happens – Julie A Fast
The Brain that Changes Itself – Norman Doidge
The Mind Management – Dr Steve Peters
The Universe Inside You – Brian Clegg
Make your Brain Work – Amy Brown
Keep your brain alive – Lawrence Katz and Manning Rubin

Spark: how exercise will improve the performance of your brain – Eric Hageman and Dr John J Ratey

The body has a mind of its own – Sandra Blakeslee and Matthew Blakeslee

Heal your brain – David J Hellerstein

The Everything Guide to the Human Brain – Rudolph C Hadfield PhD

Bounce – Matthew Syed

The Science of Mind – Ernest Shurleff Holmes

How the mind works – Steven Pinker

Daring greatly – Brene Brown

Origins of Neurolinguistic programming - John Grinder and Frank Pucelik

www.ingramcontent.com/pod-product-compliance
Lightning Source LLC
Chambersburg PA
CBHW022109090426
42743CB00008B/773